Pas à Pas en Français

Third Level
French Grammar

Eugene O'Sullivan

FOLENS

Printed in Ireland at the press of the publishers 1993

Folens Publishers,
Airton Road,
Tallaght,
Dublin 24.

ISBN 0 86121 4684

Editor
Rachel O'Connor

All rights reserved. No part of this publication may be reproduced, stored in a retrieval system, or transmitted in any form, or by any means, electronic, mechanical, photocopying, recording, or otherwise, without the prior written permission of the publishers.

This book is sold subject to the conditions that it shall not, by way of trade or otherwise, be lent, re-sold, hired out or otherwise circulated without the publisher's prior consent in any form of binding or cover other than that in which it is published and without a similar condition including this condition being imposed on the subsequent purchaser.

CONTENTS

Introduction 5

Acknowledgements 6

INTRODUCTORY LESSON

Lesson 1   Parts of Speech   7

THE VERB

Lesson 2   Verb Tenses   11

Lesson 3   Three Conjugations of Verbs   14
Present Tense
Basic Past Tense (passé composé) using *Avoir*

Lesson 4   Passé Composé using *Être*   18

Lesson 5   Imperfect Tense   22
Deciding whether to use Passé Composé or Imperfect

Lesson 6   The Negative   25
The Imperative

Lesson 7   Pluperfect Tense   29
Venir de Construction
Past Historic Tense

Lesson 8   Future Tense   34
Immediate Future
Conditional Tense

Lesson 9   Past Conditional Tense   38
Conditional Sentences using *Si*

Lesson 10   Questions   40
Inversion

Lesson 11   Use of *Depuis* and Similar Constructions   45

Lesson 12   Passive Voice   48
Use of *On*

Lesson 13   Present Partciple   51
Perfect Infinitive after *Après*

Lesson 14   The Subjunctive Mood   54
Verbal Constructions followed by Subjunctive

Lesson 15   Conjunctions followed by Subjunctive   58
Relative Pronoun Constructions followed by Subjunctive

THE PRONOUN

Lesson 16	Direct and Indirect Object Pronouns	61
Lesson 17	Relative Pronouns	66
Lesson 18	Stressed Pronouns Other Object Pronouns : *Y* and *En* Position and Order of Object Pronouns	71

OTHER PARTS OF SPEECH

Lesson 19	Agreement and Position of Adjectives Possessive Adjectives	76
Lesson 20	Past Participle Agreement	81
Lesson 21	The Article	85
Lesson 22	Formation of Adverbs Comparative and Superlative of Adjectives and Adverbs	88
Lesson 23	Prepositions	92

APPENDICES

Appendix A	Irregular Verbs (tables + index)	100
Appendix B	Verbs Easily Confused	111
Appendix C	*-er* Verbs with Variations in Spelling	112
Appendix D	*Devoir* and *Pouvoir*	115
Appendix E	Expressions with *Avoir* and *Faire*	117
Appendix F	Numbers	118
Appendix G	Expletive *Ne* with Subjunctive	119
Appendix H	Use of Reflexive Verbs to Translate English Passive	120
Appendix I	Additional Examples of Inversion	121
Appendix J	Additional Tenses	122
Appendix K	Demonstrative Pronouns and Possessive Pronouns	124
Index		126

INTRODUCTION

This grammar course has been specially designed to meet the needs of students who require a knowledge of a certain amount of basic French grammar in order to prepare for the Honours Level Leaving Certificate Examination or to proceed with French language studies at third level.

Because an oral-based communicative method has been the recommended approach in Irish secondary schools for several years now, many students will have reached sixth year, or chosen to study French at university, with only a very limited knowledge of the grammatical structure of the language. A typical student may not know, for example, what exactly is the difference between the relative pronouns *qui* and *que*, when to use a direct or indirect object pronoun, or which constructions involve the use of the subjunctive mood of the verb. This course is intended as an opportunity to become acquainted with some of the more important rules of French grammar, because without this knowledge one would find it very difficult to do well either in the Honours Leaving Cert or in university French examinations.

It is worth pointing out that what has just been said represents only half of the picture. Students leaving school today have a tremendous advantage over students of a number of years ago in the areas of oral and aural proficiency and in the wide range of texts from newspapers, magazines, advertising and literature which they have studied. However, an awareness of the structures of French grammar is vital in order to channel all these skills and this experience towards success in examinations where correct written French is expected.

The presentation of grammar in this book is such that it presupposes no previous knowledge of grammatical terminology and jargon. Consequently, most parts of this course would be ideally suited to teachers of French to Honours Leaving Cert classes who may feel the need to provide their students with adequate grammatical "back-up". Alternatively, with its clear step-by-step approach, this book meets the needs of individual students who wish to supplement or complement the French that they learn in class.

Students may wish to note that Appendix A provides tables of over 50 different French irregular verbs (in order of importance) and an index of 190 irregular verbs, any part of which may be obtained from the tables. For the sake of clarity, accents have been placed on capital letters in this course, although this is contrary to normal French practice.

This present textbook is the third edition of a grammar course which has been taught in the Department of French, University College, Cork, since 1991. The course is divided into 23 lessons, one of which is studied in class each week during the academic year, to make up Unit 102 of the First Arts French programme. All the lessons dealing with verbal constructions have been grouped together at the beginning, but students are encouraged to consult the other sections of the course according as specific problems may arise in their weekly translations. Your attention is drawn in particular to the table of contents, the reference index at the end, and the eleven appendices, of which A, B, C and F should be consulted regularly. In fact, students find that any extra work they put into Unit 102 in First Year puts them in a better position to benefit from Unit 101 (Translation and Free Composition) and from the language courses offered in subsequent years.

On the basis of experience acquired in teaching French at UCC, students are strongly advised to read through each lesson before attending the grammar class based on that lesson, and they are given an opportunity to attempt the translation exercises accompanying each lesson during the second half of the class. Coping successfully with the exercises on one's own is the only way to ensure that one has mastered the main points of the lesson. It is recommended that the content of the lesson be revised thoroughly at some time during the 48 hours following the class.

ACKNOWLEDGEMENTS

I wish to express my gratitude to those who taught me French grammar and translation at Coláiste na Rinne, St Augustine's College, Dungarvan, and UCC, including Mr Patrick Keevers, Mme Martine Seda, Prof. Matthew Mac Namara and Prof. Kathleen O'Flaherty.

Thanks are due to Dr Grace Neville for encouraging me to proceed with the production of this manual and to Prof. Robert Pickering for giving it an opportunity to prove itself in 1991. Helpful advice was received from many members of the staff of the Department of French, in particular Ms Sylvie Campion, Dr Maeve Conrick, Ms Kathleen Hoctor, Ms Ita Morrissey and Mr Cathal Ó Corcora, which made it possible to modify and improve this course after its trial run, with the aim of making it as accessible as possible to students.

Ms Eileen Casey and Ms Joan McKeating were of invaluable assistance during the production of the first two editions with their guidance as to the use of word processor and printer.

Eugene O'Sullivan
January 1993

LESSON 1

PARTS OF SPEECH

Every word in a sentence belongs to one of eight basic categories, depending on what function it has in the sentence. These eight categories are called the "parts of speech" and the ability to decide which part of speech a word represents is the most basic step in understanding the grammatical structure of a sentence and in setting out to translate from one language to another in an organised way.

(1) NOUN

(Simple definition : the name of a person, place or thing)

Nouns include all names of people and places (called "proper nouns", e.g. John, Catherine, France, Ireland, Cork) and any word which can be preceded by **the** in English, e.g. paper, door, coat, finger, dog, house, love, courage, quantity, collection, attempt.

In French, every noun is either masculine or feminine, and the gender of the noun must be established before it is used in a sentence.

(2) VERB

(Simple definition : the action word in the sentence)

The verb denotes the action which is presented in the sentence, e.g. runs, dropped, threw, bites, pushes, break, hide. As well as actions, verbs also present states or processes, e.g. to stay, to know, to be, to think, to dislike, to lie. In French, as in English, a verb may consist of just one word, or it may include two or three words : will find, was drinking, would speak, had been seen, would have liked, has been forgotten.

(3) ADJECTIVE

An adjective is a word that qualifies (i.e. describes, tells us more about) a noun. Any word that describes your dog, or your notebook, or your sister, or the room you're sitting in, is an adjective, e.g. big, black, friendly, warm, untidy, this, our, smelly, Irish, attractive, rectangular, third.

Because adjectives are usually linked so closely to one particular noun, this will determine their form (spelling of the ending) and their position in French.

(4) ADVERB

An adverb is a word that modifies a verb. This means that it tells us more about (or fills in background information to) the action or state presented in the verb. Most adverbs answer the questions where? when? and how?

For example: **where?** - here, everywhere, abroad, nearby, overhead.
              when? - yesterday, tomorrow, now, often, soon, then, afterwards, before.
              how? - together, well, slowly, carefully, bravely, politely.

(**NB** These last adverbs ending in *-ly* were formed from adjectives : *slow, careful, brave, polite*. The most common way to make an adverb is to form it from an adjective.)

As well as helping to define the meaning of verbs, some adverbs modify the meaning of adjectives. The word *strange* is an adjective, and words like very, rather, so, too and less, which can precede it, are included in the category of adverbs. These five examples could also be used with the adverb *strangely*, so that the full definition of an adverb is :
    any word which modifies a verb, an adjective or another adverb.

Because adverbs are usually linked so closely to one of the other words in the sentence, this will determine their position in French.

(5) PRONOUN

Pronouns are words used to replace nouns, to avoid repeating the same nouns too often. The most common pronouns are those used to replace people's names : I, me, you, he, she, him, her, we, us, they, them. All these, and also the word **it**, are called Personal Pronouns.

Words like *who, which* and *that* are used to replace a noun when linking up two short sentences to form a longer sentence. These are called Relative Pronouns.

For example: Tom loves Mary. Mary has long hair. → Tom loves Mary, *who* has long hair.

(6) PREPOSITION

These words show the relationship of one noun or pronoun to another.
They include :   to, from, by, with, for, of, without;
             words that denote position : on, under, in, beside, near, above, over, through;
             words that express relationship in time : before, after, during, since, until.

Note that all these words would usually precede a noun or pronoun, e.g. with my brother, at our house, beside the chair, from us, before the holidays.

We will find that, in French, prepositions like *à* and *de* are also used to link verbs and adjectives into the structure of a sentence.

(7) CONJUNCTION

These are words which link two parts of a sentence together, or which link two words together within the sentence.

For example: dogs *and* cats, small *but* strong, he *or* she.
               I went there *because* (*although* / *before*) I was afraid.
              They will speak to him *when* (*if* / *provided*) he sits down.
              I was happy *before* I met you.

(8) ARTICLE

This is a word which directly precedes a noun to distinguish it from other nouns. There are two kinds in English : definite article **the** and indefinite article **a** / **an**.

In French, there is also a plural indefinite article (translated as **some** books, **some** horses) and a partitive article, which expresses the idea " a certain amount of ".

It is worth noting that in many cases, the decision as to which of the eight categories a word falls into depends on the context. For example, you may have noticed on the previous page (if you were awake) that the word *before* is classified as a preposition when it introduces a noun or a pronoun (*before* the holidays), and as a conjunction when it introduces a verb (*before* I met you). It is an adverb when it answers the question "when?" (I have been here *before*).

The words *light* and *that* are just as versatile :

Turn on the *light* in the hall.	**(noun)**
We *light* the fire at five every day.	**(verb)**
Your bag is very *light* today.	**(adjective)**

That book belongs to me.	**(adjective)**	: describing the book)
It was he who bought *that*.	**(pronoun**	: replacing some noun)
I know *that* she is in there.	**(conjunction**	: linking the two verbs)

Being aware that a word may act as several different parts of speech will be vitally important when learning to use a dictionary properly.

— EXERCISE A —

Read the following passage and decide which part of speech each of the words is.

Note: There are three examples of a verb consisting of two words. To avoid confusion, five of the words which might present difficulties have been categorised for you : [1] = adjective. You should end up with 20 nouns, 7 verbs, 12 adjectives, 2 adverbs, 3 pronouns, 13 prepositions, 2 conjunctions and 13 articles.

Along the Mardyke the trees were in bloom. They entered the grounds of the college and were led by the garrulous porter across the quadrangle. But their progress across the gravel was brought to a halt after every[1] ten[1] paces by some[1] reply of the porter's. During these halts, Stephen stood awkwardly behind the two[1] men, weary of the subject. The lively southern speech which had entertained him all[1] the morning now irritated his ears.

James Joyce, *A Portrait of the Artist as a Young Man*
(adapted slightly)

— EXERCISE B —

Read the following passage and identify which part of speech each of the words is.

Note that there is one example of a verb consisting of two words. For the purpose of this exercise, *d'habitude* and *d'emblée* should be regarded as single words. To avoid confusion, three words have again been categorised for you : ² = adverb; ³ = preposition. You should end up with 10 nouns, 12 verbs (including infinitives and present participles with *en*), 5 adjectives, 6 adverbs, 8 pronouns, 8 prepositions, 2 conjunctions and 7 articles.

Il alluma une cigarette d'une main tremblante, et reprit sa promenade. La mort bien bête qui venait de passer si près² de lui avait embrouillé les fils qui l'attachaient d'habitude à la réalité. Puis il se dit en³ souriant que le hasard venait d'honorer son talent de policier en³ lui faisant rencontrer d'emblée l'assassin local.

Pascal Lainé, *Trois petits meurtres ... et puis s'en va*
(adapted slightly)

NB *reprendre* : (here) to resume
    venir + de : to have just done something
    embrouiller : to tangle, muddle
    un fil : a thread
    le hasard : fate
    d'emblée : straight away

LESSON 2

VERB TENSES

When you set out to write a sentence in French, the most important decision to make is how to handle the verb. If you make a mistake in the form of the verb, either the sentence won't make sense, or else the meaning will be changed completely, so your priority must be to find the correct verbal construction in French. To achieve this, you must be able to examine the verb in English in order to decide what the French equivalent is.

As it happens, the systems of tenses in English and French are very similar, so that usually, if you can identify what tense is being used in English, that tells you what to do in French. Being able to identify the tense means being very clear in your mind as to the distinction between "they were killing" and "they were killed", or "she has wounded" and "she was wounded". In order to help you to distinguish between the seven basic tenses in French, we shall begin our study of the verb by setting out the meaning of these tenses in English, before we see how to form them in French.

Here is a list of the meanings of the seven basic French tenses of the verb 'to eat', with 'he' (3rd person singular) as subject:

Present (présent)		he eats, he is eating
	Perfect (passé composé)	he has eaten he ate (the action was fully completed)
Past	**Imperfect** (imparfait)	he was eating, he used to eat he ate (the action was repeated an indefinite number of times)
	Pluperfect (plus-que-parfait)	he had eaten
Future (futur)		he will eat
Conditional (conditionnel)		he would eat
Past Conditional (conditionnel du passé)		he would have eaten

In all of these tenses above, the subject of the verb (he) is doing the action. There is an equivalent for each of these tenses, in the situation where, instead of doing the action, *he* is in the unhappy position of *being eaten*. The term in grammar for this second set of tenses is the **passive voice**, as opposed to the **active voice** above.

Present Passive	he is eaten, he is being eaten
Past → Perfect Passive	he has been eaten he was eaten (the action was fully completed)
Past → Imperfect Passive	he was being eaten, he used to be eaten he was eaten (the action was repeated an indefinite number of times)
Past ⇢ Pluperfect Passive	he had been eaten
Future Passive	he will be eaten
Conditional Passive	he would be eaten
Past Conditional Passive	he would have been eaten

Study these lists carefully and this will help you to see the differences in meaning.

You should be able to see now that "they were killing" is the *imperfect tense* (like "he was eating") but "they were killed" is *passive*, probably perfect tense (like "he was eaten").

Again "she has wounded" is *perfect tense* (like "he has eaten") but "she was wounded" is *passive*, probably perfect tense (like "he was eaten").

NB Several French tenses, which are not essential in order to be able to write basic French, are not dealt with in this lesson. These include the *past historic* (same meaning as the basic English past tense) and the *past anterior* (same meaning as the pluperfect), both of which are only used in formal literary French and not in everyday speech, and also the *future perfect* ("he will have eaten"). Part of lesson 7 will deal with how to form the past historic tense; for the other two, see Appendix J.

— EXERCISE A —

Identify the tense of each of the highlighted verbs. Remember that you are dealing with a Passive Voice Tense whenever the subject of the verb is at the receiving end of the action.

(1) We **were forgetting** them, but somebody **reminded** us.
(2) Every time they **used to give** a prize, we **were forgotten**.
(3) When the time **came** to award the prizes yesterday, we **were forgotten**.
(4) You **saw** them last Thursday.
(5) You **had seen** them the previous Thursday too.
(6) You **have seen** them already.

(7) You **have been seen** at the cinema with these people.
(8) I **would have paid** him more than that.
(9) I **would be paid** at least £20 for doing that.
(10) The students **are reading** in the library.
(11) The parish notices **are read** out in church every Sunday.

— EXERCISE B —

Make a copy of the chart which follows and fill in on it all the basic tenses of the verb *to buy* (*in English*) with **we** as subject.

You should include, for example, *we were buying, we will be bought, we would have bought,* etc.

Present (présent)	
Past → **Perfect** (passé composé) / **Imperfect** (imparfait) / **Pluperfect** (plus-que-parfait)	
Future (futur)	
Conditional (conditionnel)	
Past Conditional (conditionnel du passé)	

Present Passive	
Past → **Perfect Passive** / **Imperfect Passive** / **Pluperfect Passive**	
Future Passive	
Conditional Passive	
Past Conditional Passive	

LESSON 3

THREE CONJUGATIONS OF VERBS
PRESENT TENSE
BASIC PAST TENSE (passé composé) USING *AVOIR*

IRREGULAR VERBS

French verbs are either regular or irregular. To be able to use an irregular verb, you must learn a certain number of parts. In order to form the basic tenses listed in the previous lesson, you need to know :

  (1) all the present tense, i.e. six bits,
  (2) the past participle,
  (3) the stem of the future tense. (See Lesson 8.)

These key parts will enable you to get all the other parts of the verb. Appendix A (pp.100 - 105) lists the key parts of all French irregular verbs except for a handful which are no longer found in the living language. You should set about learning these verbs in a gradual way as soon as possible.

REGULAR VERBS

The regular verbs fall into three divisions (called "conjugations") depending on the ending of the infinitive (the name of the verb). Most verbs have an infinitive ending in *-er* (e.g. donner), others in *-ir* (e.g. finir) and others in *-re* (e.g. vendre).

To put a regular verb into the various tenses, you need to know *three sets of endings* (for present, imperfect and future tenses) and you must understand how to use *compound tenses*. These are tenses with two parts :

  (1) an auxiliary verb which will be either *avoir* or *être*,
  (2) the past participle.

PRESENT TENSE - FORMATION

The only tense with a different set of endings for each of the three conjugations is the present, which means that it is particularly important to remember which type of verb you're dealing with when getting the present tense (or any other part of the verb derived from the present).

The three sets of present tense endings are as follows :

  -er verbs : -e, -es, -e, -ons, -ez, -ent.
  -ir verbs : -is, -is, -it, -issons, -issez, -issent.
  -re verbs : -s, -s, –, -ons, -ez, -ent.

For example:

	Donner		Finir		Vendre
	je donne		je finis		je vends
	tu donnes		tu finis		tu vends
	il / elle donne		il / elle finit		il / elle vend
	nous donnons		nous finissons		nous vendons
	vous donnez		vous finissez		vous vendez
	ils / elles donnent		ils / elles finissent		ils / elles vendent

NB (i) The *-iss-* syllable in the plural of *-ir* verbs.
    (ii) The *-es* ending of the tu form of *-er* verbs.
    (iii) The final *-ent* of the 3rd person plural is always silent.
    (iv) For each of the three types, the three forms of the singular are pronounced exactly the same.

PRESENT TENSE - MORE THAN ONE MEANING

Any French present tense form can have at least three different meanings in English.
For example: *nous rencontrons* : we meet, we are meeting, we do meet.
              il va : he goes, he is going, he does go.

So if you want to say "I am meeting", "they are eating", "she is falling" or "you are choosing" in French, what you need is simply the ordinary present tense, without using any form of the verb "to be" (être).

    I am meeting → je rencontre   they are eating → ils mangent
    she is falling → elle tombe   you are choosing → vous choisissez

PASSÉ COMPOSÉ

In the past tense, the most basic way to say "I gave" is to use the form "I have given" → j'ai donné.

Similarly "he saw" → "he has seen" → il a vu,
     "we forgot" → "we have forgotten" → nous avons oublié.

As you can see, this tense, which is called the *Passé Composé*, has *two parts* to the verb : the present tense of the verb *avoir* "to have" (called the auxiliary verb) and the *past participle* (defined on the next page).

The past participle of an -er verb ends in -é (donné, regardé, fermé),
                    -ir verb → -i (fini, choisi, puni),
                    -re verb → -u (vendu, entendu, perdu).

The full past tense (passé composé) of *penser* is :

> j'ai pensé   nous avons pensé
> tu as pensé   vous avez pensé
> il / elle a pensé   ils /elles ont pensé

Similarly for *attendre* :

> j'ai attendu   nous avons attendu
> tu as attendu   vous avez attendu
> il / elle a attendu   ils / elles ont attendu

In order to put any irregular verb in the past tense, one must first learn the irregular past participle.

For example: *He took* (prendre : pris)   → Il a pris

You followed (suivre : suivi) → Vous avez suivi

The past participle may be defined as that word in the sentence which tells you the state something is in, after the action of the verb has been performed on it.

For example: broken, lost, forgotten, improved, polished, torn.

> The police found the car, *upturned* on the roadside.
> Once the job was *done*, everyone was happy.

In English, the past participle is very often found following some part of the verb "to have". He has *seen*, they hadn't *found*, having *been*.

Present tense in French always has just **one** word for the verb; whether you want to say she *shouts* or she *is shouting*, the French will be *elle crie*.

Passé Composé always has **two** parts to the verb; whether it translates we *saw* or we *have seen*, the French will be *nous avons vu*.

— EXERCISE —

Translate the following :

(1) they are blushing
(2) they blushed
(3) they blush
(4) I sold
(5) I sell
(6) I have sold
(7) you have finished *
(8) you are finishing *
(9) we have got thin
(10) we are getting thin
(11) you are eating *
(12) you have eaten *
(13) you heard *
(14) you hear *
(15) he is waiting
(16) he waited
(17) we are choosing
(18) we chose
(19) we choose
(20) she closes
(21) she closed
(22) they have lost
(23) they lose
(24) I met
(25) I meet
(26) I am meeting
(27) they have got old
(28) they are getting old

* Tu and vous forms

The verbs you will need are :

attendre, choisir, entendre, fermer, finir, maigrir, manger, perdre, rencontrer, rougir, vendre, vieillir.

LESSON 4

PASSÉ COMPOSÉ USING *ÊTRE*

There are two groups of French verbs that don't use *avoir* as the auxiliary verb to form the passé composé (and all the other compound tenses).

INTRANSITIVE VERBS OF MOTION

The first group is made up of verbs of motion which do not take a direct object (See p.61), i.e. they are "intransitive". It consists of a list of twelve verbs of *going and coming* :

Aller	Arriver	Descendre	Entrer
Monter	Mourir	Naître	Partir
Rester	Sortir	Tomber	Venir

plus **Retourner** and **Passer** when they don't have an object,
plus compounds of the verbs above, e.g. **Rentrer**, **Devenir**, **Parvenir**, etc.

Instead of *avoir*, these verbs use the present tense of *être* with the past participle to form the basic past tense.

Please note that the above list, which it is vital to learn by heart, does not include all "verbs of motion"; courir (to run) and suivre (to follow), for example, use *avoir*. The distinction between partir (to leave, to go away) and sortir (to go out, to come out) should also be noted.

NB Three of the verbs on the above list have an irregular past participle :

mourir → **mort** ; naître → **né** ; venir → **venu**.

All the others form their past participle regularly.

The past participle of these verbs agrees with its subject just as an adjective agrees with a noun, taking *-e* if feminine and *-s* if plural. (Past participles of all the other verbs which use *avoir* to form the passé composé do not agree with their subject. See Lesson 20.)

In the following example, the spelling of the past participle for the first and second persons would depend on whether the *je, tu, nous* or *vous* involved is masculine or feminine, and whether the *vous* is singular or plural :

Je suis resté / restée	Nous sommes restés / restées
Tu es resté / restée	Vous êtes resté / restée / restés / restées
Il est resté	Ils sont restés
Elle est restée	Elles sont restées

NB As regards agreement, any combination of masculine and feminine is regarded as masculine plural.

For example: Charles et ses huit soeurs sont venus me rendre visite.

Complication :

All of these *être* verbs are verbs of movement (or lack of movement in the case of *rester*). Although they are normally intransitive, a few of them can be used with a direct object (as *transitive* verbs); when this happens they use *avoir* rather than *être* as their auxiliary verb, and their past participles do not agree with the subject.

For example: We went up. → Nous sommes montés.
   We brought the books up to my bedroom.
      → Nous avons monté les livres dans ma chambre.
   She went out. → Elle est sortie.
   She took out her handkerchief.
      → Elle a sorti son mouchoir.

i.e. In the constructions "descendre quelque chose", "monter quelque chose", "rentrer quelque chose" and "sortir quelque chose", these verbs use *avoir* to form the passé composé. The same applies to "retourner quelque chose" and "passer quelque chose".

REFLEXIVE VERBS

The second group of verbs using *être* rather than *avoir* to form the passé composé are verbs that include the reflexive pronoun *me, te, se,* etc. They normally involve actions that one does to oneself, or something that people do to one another, e.g. *se peigner* (to comb one's hair) and *s'écrire* (to write to one another).

In the present tense, the verb endings of a reflexive verb depend on whether it is an *-er, -ir, -re* or irregular verb.
There are three bits: (1) subject pronoun *je, tu* .., (2) reflexive pronoun *me, te* .., (3) verb.

Present Tense of *se laver* :	je me lave	nous nous lavons
	tu te laves	vous vous lavez
	il / elle se lave	ils / elles se lavent
Present Tense of *se détendre* :	je me détends	nous nous détendons
	tu te détends	vous vous détendez
	il / elle se détend	ils / elles se détendent
Present Tense of *s'habiller* :	je m'habille	nous nous habillons
	tu t'habilles	vous vous habillez
	il / elle s'habille	ils / elles s'habillent

In the passé composé, other verbs have three parts including the subject (e.g. il a trouvé, nous sommes arrivés). Reflexive verbs include the reflexive pronoun *me, te, se* and so they have four parts. Their past participles usually **seem** to agree with the subject. (See Lesson 20 p. 81 for the full explanation of this point).

Passé Composé of *se laver* :

je me suis lavé(e)	nous nous sommes lavé(e)s
tu t' es lavé(e)	vous vous êtes lavé(e)(s)
il s' est lavé	ils se sont lavés
elle s' est lavée	elles se sont lavées

NB It is very important to make sure to learn by heart this model of the past tense of a reflexive verb. If you cannot use this part of the verb easily, you will have great difficulty in making it negative (Lesson 6) and putting it in the form of a question (Lesson 10).

SUMMARY

The vast majority of French verbs use *Avoir* to form the passé composé. So do a few of the "être verbs" when they take an object. With *avoir* the past participle does not agree with the subject.

   e.g. Elle a mangé la viande. Nous avons trouvé les ballons.

The verbs listed on p.18 use *Être* to form the passé composé. With *être* the past participle agrees with the subject,

   e.g. Elle est arrivée. Nous sommes venus.

All reflexive verbs use *Être* to form the passé composé. The past participle of a reflexive verb **seems** to agree with the subject. (This is explained fully in Lesson 20.)

   e.g. Elle s'est peignée. Nous nous sommes battus.

— EXERCISE —

Translate the following sentences, using the *passé composé* each time:

(1) The birds flew away.
(2) We stayed at home.
(3) You were born in France.
(4) I went down the street.
(5) I went down very quickly.
(6) We hurried.
(7) She picked her blue dress for the party.
(8) She left two days later.
(9) They stopped at three o' clock.
(10) They showed the book to the teacher.
(11) She went up to her bedroom.
(12) She went up the steps. (les marches)
(13) I stood up.
(14) They went out into the street.
(15) You both got up early this morning.
   [*both* : tous les deux (after verb); toutes les deux (if feminine)]
(16) Yvonne sat down on the small chair.
(17) Yvonne and Claire sat down on the small chairs.
(18) Yvonne, Claire and Gaston sat down on the small chairs.
(19) We became teachers in the same town.
(20) We both taught French.

The verbs you will need are :

s'arrêter, s'asseoir (p.p. assis), choisir, se dépêcher, descendre, devenir, enseigner, s'envoler, se lever, monter, montrer, naître, partir, rester, sortir.

LESSON 5

IMPERFECT TENSE
DECIDING WHETHER TO USE PASSÉ COMPOSÉ OR IMPERFECT

IMPERFECT TENSE

The imperfect tense is the past tense that tells us what *used to happen* or what *was happening* in the past.

Except for *être*, all verbs form the imperfect as follows :

> Take the 1st person plural (the *nous* part) of the present tense, drop the *-ons*, and add : *-ais, -ais, -ait, -ions, -iez, -aient*.

Note that there is no *-a-* in the *nous* and *vous* endings of the imperfect, and that the other four parts are all pronounced the same.

For example: *Finir* → nous finissons → *finiss* →

je finiss*ais*	nous finiss*ions*
tu finiss*ais*	vous finiss*iez*
il / elle finiss*ait*	ils / elles finiss*aient*

Se Réveiller → nous nous réveillons → *réveill* →

je me réveill*ais*	nous nous réveill*ions*
tu te réveill*ais*	vous vous réveill*iez*
il / elle se réveill*ait*	ils / elles se réveill*aient*

The only exception is *être* : j'étais, tu étais, il / elle était,
    nous étions, vous étiez, ils / elles étaient.

The basic meaning of *nous finissions*, then, would be either "we were finishing" or "we used to finish", and *il se réveillait* could mean "he was waking up" or "he used to wake up".

DECIDING WHICH PAST TENSE TO USE

When a simple English past tense (e.g. he gave, they went, etc.) is being translated into French, the translator has to pause and think about which past tense to use in French.

The basic distinction between the two past tenses we have looked at so far is that the passé composé tells *what happened* in the past (a completed event) while the imperfect tells *the way things were* (i.e. what was in the process of happening or what used to happen).

The distinction does **not** involve the length of time the event took to happen. Very slow or lengthy events can be in the passé composé, provided they are complete.

For example: The Stone Age lasted many centuries.
→ L'âge de pierre a duré bien des siècles. (*not* durait)

(A) Passé Composé is used for narration and to tell what happened next in a series of events.

For example: Il a entendu quelqu'un frapper à la porte, a descendu l'escalier et a souri en voyant la petite fille.

It tells of a single, completed action in the past, or an action repeated a *definite* number of times to form a complete series.

For example: Chaque jour pendant une semaine, il est allé au lycée.
Plusieurs fois il a essayé, mais il n'a pas réussi à entrer.

(B) Imperfect is used to denote :

— an incompleted action or process (that was happening at some point in the past)
e.g. Quand je suis sorti de chez moi, il pleuvait et il faisait du vent.

— an habitual action or a single action repeated an indefinite number of times.
e.g. Toutes les fois qu'il me rendait visite, il m'apportait un petit cadeau.
(Whenever he **came** to visit me, he **brought** / would bring / used to bring me a small present).

— how people and things appeared in the past (description).
e.g. Mon oncle portait sa nouvelle cravate et avait l'air content.
(My uncle wore his new tie and looked happy.)

A FEW VERBS REQUIRING SPECIAL CARE :

- **Was**
  - (i) Elle était à la cuisine quand le téléphone a sonné.
    (= "was already", telling **the way things were**)
  - (ii) Elle a été très contente de me revoir.
    (= "became", telling **what happened**)

- **There was**
  - (i) Il y avait un arbre au milieu du champ.
    (= "existed", telling **the way things were**)
  - (ii) Soudain, il y a eu un cri.
    (= "occurred", telling **what happened**)

- **Could**
  - (i) A l'âge de dix ans, il pouvait soulever cette pierre.
    (= "was already able to", telling **the way things were**)
  - (ii) Il a allumé la lampe et a pu voir que sa femme pleurait.
    (= "was enabled to", telling **what happened**)

- **Had**
  - (i) Elle n'a pas acheté ce journal, parce qu'elle l'avait déjà.
    (= "was already in possession of", telling **the way things were**)
  - (ii) Heureusement, elle a eu le temps de s'échapper.
    (= "received / got", telling **what happened**)

- **Knew**
  - (i) Il n'a pas regardé le texte, car il le savait par coeur.
    (= "knew already", telling **the way things were**)
  - (ii) A ce moment-là, il a su qu'on le détestait.
    (= "became aware / realised", telling **what happened**)

> **Basic Disctinction :**
>
> - telling what happened in the past → *Passé Composé*
> - telling the way things were in the past → *Imperfect*

NB This problem only arises when translating the simple English past tense, e.g. he broke the law, they broke the law, etc.

has broken / have broken → *passé composé*

was breaking / were breaking / used to break → imperfect

— EXERCISE —

Translate the following sentences, paying careful attention to the choice of past tense in each case:

(1) They used to wear expensive clothes when they were rich.
(2) I was drinking my coffee when they entered[A] the room.
(3) The game[B] of tennis lasted five hours.
(4) We were surprised[C] when he phoned us.
(5) We were watching television when he phoned us.
(6) When she saw the big dog, she was afraid.
(7) Whenever[D] I met them, they were having a good time[E].
(8) Suddenly I knew that he didn't like me and I cried[F].
(9) I remember[G] that you cried[F] whenever[D] he got cross[H].
(10) There was an accident in front of the church yesterday.
(11) She used to choose this wine when they invited me to dinner.
(12) I drove to his house several times, but he wasn't there.
(13) I was disappointed[I] when I read your letter.

A : entrer *dans*   **B** : une partie   **C** : être surpris   **D** : toutes les fois que   **E** : s'amuser
F : pleurer   **G** : se souvenir   **H** : se fâcher   **I** : être deçu

LESSON 6

THE NEGATIVE
THE IMPERATIVE

THE NEGATIVE

To form the negative of any simple tense (i.e. one part to the verb, like present and imperfect) put *ne* before the verb and *pas* after it. *Ne* will become *n'* before a vowel or h mute.

For example: J'apprends le français. → Je *n'* apprends *pas* le français.

To form the negative of the passé composé (or any other compound tense, i.e. two parts to the verb) put the *ne* and *pas* around the auxiliary verb, i.e. around the *avoir* or *être*.

For example: J'ai appris le français. → Je *n'* ai *pas* appris le français.
             Ils sont restés en France. → Ils *ne* sont *pas* restés en France.

To put the infinitive in the negative, put the *ne* and *pas* together in front of it.

For example: J'aime mieux *ne pas* aller à Londres. (I prefer not to go to London.)
             Il a décidé de *ne pas* sortir. (He decided not to go out.)

The most important negative words (all used with *ne*) include :

- **Jamais** (never)   → Il ne boit jamais d'alcool.

- **Plus** (no longer, not any more) → Elle ne va plus à l'école.

- **Rien** (nothing)   → Ils n'ont rien vu.

- **Personne** (nobody)   → Il n'y avait personne là-bas.

- **Que** (only : ne + que = seulement) → Je ne vois que lui.

- **Ni .. Ni ..** (neither A nor B) → Je ne parle ni français ni allemand.

- **Aucun(e)** (none, not any)   → Nous n'avons aucun livre.
                                      Nous n'avons aucune tasse.

(Aucun is the only one of these negative words to agree as an adjective.)

Several combinations of these negative words are possible, except that *pas* cannot occur with any of the others.

For example: Elle n'oublie jamais rien.
             Il ne rencontre plus personne.

There are a few other negative words, which are not as common as those listed, including :
- ne + point (not at all) → Elle n'aime point les chiens de Marie.
- ne + guère (hardly) → Je n'ai guère commencé.

Some of these negative words can act as subject, coming first in the sentence. When this happens, there will be a *ne* before the verb, but no *pas* after it, because the *ne* is balanced by the negative word at the beginning.

For example: Rien ne marche ici. (Nothing works around here.)
Aucun de ces films ne me plaît. (I don't like any of those films.)
Personne n'aime cette fille. (Nobody likes that girl.)

In the passé composé (and the other compound tenses), words like *plus, jamais, rien* and *guère* occur in the same position as *pas*, i.e. directly after the *avoir* or *être* (and before the past participle), but *personne* and *que* (meaning **only**) follow the past participle :

For example: Nous n'avons entendu personne.
Ils n'ont vu que mes deux frères.

Study carefully these examples of the negative of the passé composé, especially for the reflexive verb where the reflexive pronoun (me, te, se, etc.) always remains directly in front of the auxiliary verb.

FINIR

je n'ai pas fini	nous n'avons pas fini
tu n'as pas fini	vous n'avez pas fini
il n'a pas fini	ils n'ont pas fini
elle n'a pas fini	elles n'ont pas fini

SE LAVER

je ne me suis pas lavé	nous ne nous sommes pas lavés
tu ne t'es pas lavé	vous ne vous êtes pas lavés
il ne s'est pas lavé	ils ne se sont pas lavés
elle ne s'est pas lavée	elles ne se sont pas lavées

THE IMPERATIVE

This is the part of the verb used to give orders. To form a command, take the *tu* part, or the *vous* part of the Present Tense, and leave out the pronoun tu or vous :

    tu choisis → choisis !   tu viens → viens !
    vous choisissez → choisissez !   vous venez → venez !

In the case of -er verbs, including aller, the *tu* form ends in *-s*, but this *-s* is dropped in the imperative :

    tu manges → mange !
    tu vas → va !

The *nous* part of the Present Tense, without the pronoun *nous* itself, is called the 1st person plural imperative, meaning "let's —"

For example: Allons ! (let us go)   Regardons ! (let's look)

For a reflexive verb, the reflexive pronoun is included in the imperative, but *tu* becomes *toi*. These imperatives include a hyphen.

For example: *Se Laver* :   lave-toi, lavons-nous, lavez-vous.
               Se Coucher : couche-toi, couchons-nous, couchez-vous.

> Hence the imperative form of the verb consists of *one single word* if the verb is not reflexive, and two words for a reflexive verb.

There are just a few irregular verbs which do not derive their imperative forms directly from the present tense.

Être	Avoir	Savoir	Vouloir
sois	aie	sache	veuille
soyons	ayons	sachons	—
soyez	ayez	sachez	veuillez

For the imperative negative of an ordinary verb, just put *ne* and *pas* around the verb.
For example: Don't drink that. → Ne bois pas cela.
               Let's not leave yet. → Ne partons pas encore.

For the imperative negative of a reflexive verb, the reflexive pronoun comes before the verb, following the rules for the position of pronoun objects which are given in Lesson 18, pp.74 and 75.

For example: Don't be in any hurry. → Ne te presse pas.
                                                 Ne vous pressez pas.

— EXERCISE —

Translate the following sentences:

(1) They never go to mass. (à la messe)
(2) They have never gone to mass in this church.
(3) She tried not to laugh.
(4) She no longer tried to laugh.
(5) We don't see anybody near the tree.
(6) Nobody was able to go to the party.
(7) I only ate two small cakes.
(8) They didn't wake up when I shouted. (se réveiller)
(9) Drive slowly. *
(10) Hurry up ! *
(11) Don't be afraid. *
(12) Never be late for your French classes. *
(13) She didn't find anything.
(14) None of the dresses were big enough for her.
(15) I didn't speak to anybody.
(16) You didn't go to bed last night. (se coucher)
(17) Tell me the truth. *
(18) Sit down on the chair. *
(19) Follow that car ! *
(20) Let's not stay here.

* Tu and vous forms.

LESSON 7

PLUPERFECT TENSE
VENIR DE CONSTRUCTION
PAST HISTORIC TENSE

PLUPERFECT TENSE

This is the third French past tense which we are going to study in this course. It tells us what 'had' happened in the past, before another more recent event in the past. It is used for an event one step further back in time than the passé composé.

Like the passé composé, the pluperfect is a *compound* tense (i.e. two parts to the verb). It is formed by *putting the auxiliary verb in the imperfect tense,* instead of in the present tense for the passé composé.

> **Pluperfect** → Imperfect Tense of Avoir / Être + Past Participle
> → translates 'had' + past participle in English

For example: J'avais vu (I had seen)
Elle avait mangé (she had eaten)
Il était tombé (he had fallen)
Nous étions arrivés (we had arrived)
Ils s'étaient habillés (they had dressed)

- The pluperfect is often used in combination with one of the other past tenses.

  For example: Il a ouvert le cadeau que sa femme lui *avait donné*.
  (He opened the present that his wife had given him.)

  Puisque j'*avais perdu* mon portefeuille, il m'a prêté de l'argent.
  (Because I had lost my wallet, he lent me some money.)

  Dès que les filles *s'étaient couchées*, les parents prenaient un verre.
  (As soon as the girls had gone to bed, the parents used to have a drink.)

- The pluperfect is used in indirect speech to present a statement which was spoken in the passé composé.

  For example: "J'ai lu ces livres." → Elle a dit qu'elle *avait lu* ces livres.
  (She said that she had read these books.)

- Sometimes the pluperfect is required in French where a simple past tense is found in English, in order to make it clear that one event happened further back in time than the other.

   For example:

   The boss wanted to know at what time they arrived.
   → Le patron voulait savoir à quelle heure ils *étaient arrivés*. (i.e. they **had** arrived)

   Ten years after we got married, I returned to the café where I first met my wife.
   → Dix ans après notre mariage, je suis retourné au café où *j'avais fait* la connaissance de ma femme. (i.e. I **had** met)

VENIR + DE CONSTRUCTION

The present tense of *venir* followed by *de* and an infinitive tells what *has just* happened in the immediate past :

Je viens de voir votre frère. → I've just seen your brother.
(Irish Phrasing : I'm just after seeing your brother.)

Ils viennent de fermer la porte. → They've just closed the door.
(Irish Phrasing : They're just after closing the door.)

Je viens	Nous venons	
Tu viens	Vous venez	+ *de* + infinitive
Il vient	Ils viennent	
Elle vient	Elles viennent	

→ what *has just* happened

Similarly, the *imperfect* tense of *venir* followed by *de* and an infinitive tells what *had just* happened at some point in the past :

Je venais de crier quand je l'ai vu.
(I had just shouted when I saw him.)
(Irish Phrasing : I was just after shouting when I saw him.)

Nous venions de descendre quand on a frappé à la porte.
(We had just come down when there was a knock on the door.)
(Irish Phrasing : We were just after coming down ...)

Je venais	Nous venions	
Tu venais	Vous veniez	+ *de* + infinitive
Il venait	Ils venaient	
Elle venait	Elles venaient	

→ what *had just* happened

When the infinitive following *venir* + *de* is a reflexive verb, the reflexive pronoun (i.e. me, te, se) will vary depending on the subject.

For example: Il vient de se lever.   but   Je viens de *me* lever,
              (He has just got up.)   Tu viens de *te* lever, etc.

              Elle venait de se taire.   but   Nous venions de nous taire,
              (She had just fallen silent.)   Vous veniez de vous taire, etc.

PAST HISTORIC TENSE

This tense is used for formal narration in literary French (e.g. novels, short stories and formal speeches). It translates the simple English past tense (I saw, you fell, he arrived, we heard, they found, etc.). It is used where the passé composé is used in informal French, to tell what happened in the past, alongside the imperfect tense which tells the way things were in the past. The past historic is never used in speech or in informal correspondence.

For **all** *-er* verbs, including *aller* and *envoyer*, remove the -er of the infinitive and add the endings :

-ai, -as, -a, -âmes, -âtes, -èrent.

For regular verbs whose infinitive ends in *-ir* or *-re*, the endings are the same:

-is, -is, -it, -îmes, -îtes, -irent.

Donner	Finir	Vendre
je donnai	je finis	je vendis
tu donnas	tu finis	tu vendis
il / elle donna	il / elle finit	il / elle vendit
nous donnâmes	nous finîmes	nous vendîmes
vous donnâtes	vous finîtes	vous vendîtes
ils / elles donnèrent	ils / elles finirent	ils / elles vendirent

For irregular verbs, the past historic tense is formed from the past participle. The general pattern is that verbs whose past participle ends in an -i- sound, replace the -i, -is, or -it with the second set of past historic endings given above. Most irregular verbs whose past participle ends in -u replace the -u with the endings :

-us, -us, -ut, -ûmes, -ûtes, -urent.

For example: **Prendre** (pris) → je pris, il prit, etc.   **Avoir** (eu)   → j'eus, il eut, etc.
              Dire (dit)   → je dis, il dit, etc.   **Recevoir** (reçu) → je reçus, il reçut, etc.

The only irregular verbs whose past historic cannot be derived from the rules above are the following (and their compounds) :

Être	Faire	Venir	
je fus	je fis	je vins	nous vînmes
il fut	il fit	tu vins	vous vîntes
ils furent	ils firent	il vint	ils vinrent

Voir	Écrire	Naître	Mourir
je vis	j'écrivis	je naquis	je mourus
il vit	il écrivit	il naquit	il mourut
ils virent	ils écrivirent	ils naquirent	ils moururent

Battre	Coudre	Vaincre	Vêtir
je battis	je cousis	je vainquis	je vêtis
il battit	il cousit	il vainquit	il vêtit
ils battirent	ils cousirent	ils vainquirent	ils vêtirent

Tenir (like venir above) : je tins, il tint, ils tinrent.
Ouvrir (+ similar verbs listed on p.102) : j'ouvris, il ouvrit, ils ouvrirent.
Conduire (+ similar verbs listed on p.102) : je conduisis, il conduisit, ils conduisirent.
Craindre (+ similar verbs listed on p.102) : je craignis, il craignit, ils craignirent.

— EXERCISE A —

Translate the following sentences, all of which require either a *venir de* construction or the *pluperfect*.

(1) She has just broken the window.
(2) She had just broken the window when we arrived.
(3) She had already broken the window when we arrived.
(4) Because I had sat on her hat, she refused to speak to me.
   (puisque)   (refuser de)
(5) I have just sat on your hat and I am very sorry.
(6) I had just sat on her hat when she entered the room.
                    (entrer dans)
(7) I believe they have just sold their house.
(8) Somebody told me that they had just sold their house.
(9) They told me that they had stayed at home.
(10) He ate the chocolate that he bought at the supermarket.

— EXERCISE B —

Change the tense in all of these verbs from the passé composé to the past historic.
All the information you need for this task is set out on pages 31 and 32.

For example: tu as fini ➜ tu finis
                nous sommes tombés ➜ nous tombâmes

(1) je suis descendu
(2) il a regardé
(3) ils se sont habillés
(4) il a vu
(5) nous avons perdu
(6) nous avons envoyé
(7) ils sont sortis
(8) j'ai dit
(9) elle est venue
(10) je me suis lavé
(11) il a écrit
(12) j'ai lu
(13) elle est allée
(14) ils ont pris
(15) il a attendu
(16) elles ont cherché
(17) ils ont battu
(18) je suis arrivé

LESSON 8

FUTURE TENSE
IMMEDIATE FUTURE
CONDITIONAL TENSE

We have already studied how to form and use five different tenses in this course. This section presents two additional tenses, and also a verbal construction which is the equivalent of a second future tense.

FORMATION OF FUTURE TENSE

The future tense is formed from the **infinitive**. Regular -er and -ir verbs add the following endings to their infinitive:

-ai, -as, -a, -ons, -ez, -ont

For example: je donner*ai*   nous donner*ons*   je finir*ai*   nous finir*ons*
                tu donner*as*   vous donner*ez*   tu finir*as*   vous finir*ez*
                il donner*a*   ils donner*ont*   il finir*a*   ils finir*ont*

Regular -re verbs drop the -e from the infinitive before adding these endings.

For example: je vendr*ai*   nous vendr*ons*
                tu vendr*as*   vous vendr*ez*
                il vendr*a*   ils vendr*ont*

Some irregular verbs form their future tense from the infinitive.

For example: prendre → je prendrai,   sortir → je sortirai.

Others have an irregular future stem, which must be learned.

For example: aller → j'irai,   venir → je viendrai.

USES OF THE FUTURE TENSE

(A) In sentences containing a **when** clause, French will have the future tense in both parts of the sentence, whenever both verbs refer logically to the future

For example: I'll tell him when I *see* him.   → I'll tell him when I **will see** him.
                                                   → Je le lui dirai quand je le verrai.

When the sun *shines*, we'll go for a swim.   → When the sun **will shine**, we'll go for a swim.
                                                     → Quand le soleil brillera, on ira se baigner.

Not only with *quand*, but also following *aussitôt que* (as soon as), *dès que* (as soon as), and *tant que* (as long as), a French sentence will have *two* future tenses if future time is implied.

For example: Tant qu'elle *restera* ici, nous ne serons pas contents.
 (As long as she stays here, we will not be happy.)

(B) Lesson 9 deals with the use of the future tense, in conjunction with the present, in one of the *si* constructions. It is important to remember that the future tense should never occur in the same part of the sentence as the word *si* (if).

For example: S'il pleut, nous ne sortirons pas. (If it rains, we won't go out.)

IMMEDIATE FUTURE

The present tense of *aller*, followed by an infinitive, is used to express what *is going to happen* in the near future. The structure is exactly the same as in English :

For example: I am going / to set the table. → Je vais / mettre le couvert.
 They are going / to kill him. → Ils vont / le tuer.

When the infinitive following *aller* is a reflexive verb, the reflexive pronoun (i.e. *me, te, se*) will vary depending on the subject.

For example: Il va *s'*asseoir là-bas, **but** Je vais *m'*asseoir là-bas,
 Nous allons *nous* asseoir là-bas, etc.

This construction also works using the **imperfect** tense of *aller*, to express what *was going to happen*.

For example: Il allait dire quelque chose.
 (He was going to say something.)
 Est-ce que tu allais prendre un repas ?
 (Were you going to have a meal ?)

Another structure used to express what will happen in the very near future is:
être sur le point de + infinitive (to be just about to).

For example: Je suis sur le point de partir. (I'm just about to leave.)
 Nous étions sur le point de partir. (We were just about to leave.)

NB Not to be confused with *venir de* (to have just done something, i.e. in the *recent past*) which was dealt with in the last lesson.

FORMATION OF CONDITIONAL TENSE

The formation of this tense (the equivalent of "would" in English) is like that of the future tense, except that the endings are different.

Take the full infinitive for regular -er and -ir verbs, the infinitive minus final -e for regular -re verbs or the irregular future stem and add the Imperfect Tense endings :

-ais, -ais, -ait, -ions, -iez, -aient.

For example: j'aimerais (I would like)   nous aimerions (we would like)
tu aimerais (you would like)   vous aimeriez (you would like)
il / elle aimerait (he / she would like)   ils / elles aimeraient (they would like)

USES OF THE CONDITIONAL

(A) The next lesson will deal with the use of the conditional tense, in conjunction with the imperfect, in one of the *si* constructions. It is important to remember that the conditional tense should never occur in the same part of the sentence as the word *si* (if).

For example: S'il pleuvait, nous ne sortirions pas.
(If it rained, we wouldn't go out.)

(B) The conditional may have to be used in certain situations where English uses an illogical past tense after the conjunctions of time listed at the top of p.35 in connection with the future tense (i.e. *quand, dès que, aussitôt que, tant que*).

For example: Ils m'ont dit de les appeler quand je *serais* prêt.
(They told me to call them when I **was** ready.)

Elle a promis de lui parler dès qu'il *arriverait*.
(She promised to speak to him as soon as he **arrived**.)

(C) An unexpected use of the conditional is after *au cas où / dans le cas où* (in case), where English uses a present tense.

For example: Je vais prendre un parapluie au cas où il *pleuvrait*.
(I'm going to take an umbrella in case it **rains**.)

Il faut nous préparer dans le cas où ils *viendraient*.
(We must get ready in case they **come**.)

(D) The conditional is sometimes used in French for statements which are presented as an allegation rather than as a fact, i.e. statements whose accuracy the speaker is unable to vouch for.

For example: It is alleged that the Allied armies are now bombing Iraq.
→ Les armées des Alliés *seraient* en train de bombarder l'Irak.

It is reported that the government intends to create more jobs.
→ Le gouvernement *aurait* l'intention de créer plus d'emplois.

> Future Tense : Infinitive + -ai, -as, -a, -ons, -ez, -ont.
> (shall/will)
>
> Conditional Tense : Infinitive + Imperfect endings
> (would) (-ais, -ais, -ait,
> -ions, -iez, -aient)

— EXERCISES —

Translate the following sentences :

(1) She will understand the problem when she is a bit older.
(2) They said that you were going to sit here.
(3) He will write to you when he has the time.
(4) He said that he would write to you when he had the time.
(5) When we go to Spain, it will be very warm.
(6) We're going to work hard in case the exams are difficult.
(7) As soon as it is warm enough, he won't wear his gloves any more.
(8) They were just about to wash up when the phone rang.
(9) They were going to wash up when the phone rang.
(10) It is reported that the White House wants to declare war.
(11) In case the doors are locked, I'm going to bring my keys.
(12) I knew that you were just about to hit me.

LESSON 9

PAST CONDITIONAL TENSE
CONDITIONAL SENTENCES USING SI

The past conditional tense is one of the three compound tenses (with the passé composé and the pluperfect) which you will be required to use if you want to master the basic structures of French.

The past conditional translates "would have" in English and it consists of *the conditional tense of avoir or être, plus the past participle.*

For example: j'aurais + mangé   il aurait + perdu
            (I would have)   (eaten)   (he would have)   (lost)

Donner	**Aller**
j'aurais donné	je serais allé(e)
tu aurais donné	tu serais allé(e)
il aurait donné	il serait allé
elle aurait donné	elle serait allée
nous aurions donné	nous serions allé(e)s
vous auriez donné	vous seriez allé(e)(s)
ils auraient donné	ils seraient allés
elles auraient donné	elles seraient allées

SI CONSTRUCTIONS

The three most common ways of constructing a sentence with 'if' are as follows :

(i) If I understand the question, I will do my best to answer it.
   Si je *comprends* la question, je *ferai* de mon mieux pour y répondre.

Si + Present ◄────► Future

(ii) If I understood the question, I would do my best to answer it.
   Si je *comprenais* la question, je *ferais* de mon mieux pour y répondre.

Si + Imperfect ◄────► Conditional

(iii) If I had understood the question, I would have done my best to answer it.
   Si *j'avais compris* la question, *j'aurais fait* de mon mieux pour y répondre.

Si + Pluperfect ◄────► Past Conditional

NB Several other combinations of tenses are possible, but the Future or the Conditional can **never** be in the same part of the sentence as the word *si* (if). There is usually a future or conditional in the other part of the sentence.

Here are three more examples :
- (i) We will go to Greece during the holidays, if we earn enough money.
  Nous *irons* en Grèce pendant les vacances, si nous *gagnons* assez d'argent.
- (ii) We would go to Greece during the holidays, if we earned enough money.
  Nous *irions* en Grèce pendant les vacances, si nous *gagnions* assez d'argent.
- (iii) We would have gone to Greece during the holidays, if we had earned enough money.
  Nous *serions allés* en Grèce pendant les vacances, si nous *avions gagné* assez d'argent.

Note that it makes no difference to the combination of tenses, whether the *si* comes in the first or second part of the sentence.

Complication :

The word *si* can also be used in the sense of "whether". When this happens, the tense following it will be exactly the same as in English.

For example: She doesn't know if he will arrive. → Elle ne sait pas s'il arrivera.
     We didn't know if he would arrive. → Nous ne savions pas s'il arriverait.

So, if the word if means *if* : no future or conditional tense can directly follow it;
but if the word if means *whether*: it may be followed by the future or conditional.

NB *Si* drops its *i* before *il* and *ils*, but not before any other vowel, for example: elle, elles, on.
→ *s'il si elle s'ils si elles si on* (or *si l'on* in formal French).

— EXERCISE —

Translate the following sentences, having first decided which combination of tenses to use for each.
1. If you (vous) open this box, you will see her ring.
2. If you (vous) opened this box, you would see her ring.
3. If you had (vous) opened this box, you would have seen her ring.
4. He would lose his way if he didn't look at the map.
   (to lose one's way : se tromper de route)
5. We don't know if he will look at the map.
6. He would have lost his way if he hadn't looked at the map.
7. He will lose his way if he doesn't look at the map.
8. She asked me if you (tu) would wait for ten minutes.
9. You (tu) would meet him if you waited for ten minutes.
10. You (tu) will meet him if you wait for ten minutes.
11. You (tu) would have met him if you had waited for ten minutes.

LESSON 10

QUESTIONS
INVERSION

There are three ways of turning a statement into a question :

(1) By raising the tone of voice at the end of the phrase and putting a question mark at the end of the written form.

For example: Elle est malade. → Elle est malade ?

This method of asking a question is quite normal and acceptable in colloquial spoken French, but for the purposes of written French it will be necessary to master both of the other methods.

(2) By putting *est-ce que* (Is it true that ..?) in front of the original statement, without altering the order of the words.

For example: Est-ce qu'elle est malade ?
Est-ce que nous avons fini ?

(3) By *inversion*, i.e. reversing the order of subject and verb within the statement. This is the formal way of denoting a question in the written language.

The present tense (question form) of *donner* is as follows:
Donnes-tu, donne-t-il, donne-t-elle, (1st pers. sing. not used)
Donnons-nous, donnez-vous, donnent-ils, donnent-elles.

Note the -t- which is only inserted between two vowels.

For example: A-t-il son livre ?   Va-t-elle chez elle ?

To make this question form negative (i.e. Aren't you giving ? Isn't he giving ? etc.) the *ne* is placed before the hyphenated question form and the *pas* after :

	(1st per. sing. not used)	Ne donnons-nous pas ?
Tu ne donnes pas →	Ne donnes-tu pas ?	Ne donnez-vous pas ?
	Ne donne-t-il pas ?	Ne donnent-ils pas ?
	Ne donne-t-elle pas ?	Ne donnent-elles pas ?

For reflexive verbs present tense question form, the reflexive pronoun (me, te, se, etc.) is brought to the front and the subject and verb then inverted :

elle se lève → se lève-t-elle ?   il se dépêche → se dépêche-t-il ?

The full present tense question form of *se reposer* is as follows :

	(1st pers. sing. not used)	Nous reposons-nous ?
Tu te reposes →	Te reposes-tu ?	Vous reposez-vous ?
	Se repose-t-il ?	Se reposent-ils ?
	Se repose-t-elle ?	Se reposent-elles ?

To make this into a negative question (i.e. Don't you wash yourself ? Doesn't he wash himself ? etc.) the *ne* is placed at the very beginning and the *pas* at the very end :

	(1st pers. sing. not used)	Ne nous lavons-nous pas ?
Tu ne te laves pas →	Ne te laves-tu pas ?	Ne vous lavez-vous pas ?
	Ne se lave-t-il pas ?	Ne se lavent-ils pas ?
	Ne se lave-t-elle pas ?	Ne se lavent-elles pas ?

A simple way of working out these inversions is to bear in mind that in each case the subject pronoun is moved from the start of the phrase to a position **directly following the verb**. This applies even with negatives and reflexive verbs. In the following examples of inversion of the passé composé, the subject pronoun moves from the start of the phrase to a position **directly following the auxiliary verb avoir or être**.

To make a question out of a verb in the passé composé, the subject pronoun and the auxiliary verb (i.e. avoir or être) are inverted and the past participle is left at the end. Here is the passé composé question form of donner :

J'ai donné →	Ai-je donné ?	Avons-nous donné ?
	As-tu donné ?	Avez-vous donné ?
	A-t-il donné ?	Ont-ils donné ?
	A-t-elle donné ?	Ont-elles donné ?

To put this into the negative (i.e. didn't I give ? didn't you give ? etc.) the *ne* and *pas* are put around the inverted hyphenated part, so that the past participle remains at the end :

Je n'ai pas donné →	N'ai-je pas donné ?	N'avons-nous pas donné ?
	N'as-tu pas donné ?	N'avez-vous pas donné ?
	N'a-t-il pas donné ?	N'ont-ils pas donné ?
	N'a-t-elle pas donné ?	N'ont-elles pas donné ?

Reflexive verb passé composé question form :

Je me suis lavé ➔ Me suis-je lavé(e) ? Nous sommes-nous lavé(e)s ?
T'es-tu lavé(e)? Vous êtes-vous lavé(e)(s) ?
S'est-il lavé ? Se sont-ils lavés ?
S'est-elle lavée ? Se sont-elles lavées ?

Reflexive verb passé composé question form **negative** :

Je ne me suis pas lavé ➔ Ne me suis-je pas lavé(e) ? Ne nous sommes-nous pas lavé(e)s ?
Ne t'es-tu pas lavé(e) ? Ne vous êtes-vous pas lavé(e)(s) ?
Ne s'est-il pas lavé ? Ne se sont-ils pas lavés ?
Ne s'est-elle pas lavée ? Ne se sont-elles pas lavées ?

NB If in doubt about the order of words in any of these cases, there is always the option of using *Est-ce que* and retaining the order of the statement.

For example: Est-ce que j'ai donné?
Est-ce que je n'ai pas donné ?
Est-ce que je me suis lavé ?
Est-ce que je ne me suis pas lavé ?

> Whatever form of the passé composé (or any other compound tense) you use, whether statement or question, positive or negative, the past participle **always** comes last.

In all of these cases so far, we have changed statements where the subject is a pronoun into questions. In order to use inversion to make a question when the subject is a noun, the noun remains in position at the start of the phrase and then the verb is inverted with a pronoun referring back to the subject. This is known as **complex inversion**.

For example: Will the doctor answer my letter ?
➔ The doctor, will he answer my letter ?
➔ Le médecin répondra-t-il à ma lettre ?

Didn't your sister enjoy herself yesterday ?
➔ Your sister, didn't she enjoy herself yesterday ?
➔ Votre soeur ne s'est-elle pas amusée hier ?

For questions beginning with words like Where ? When ? How ? Why ? either *est-ce que* or *inversion* must be used after the initial question word.

For example: Why are they doing that ? ➔ Pourquoi font-ils cela ?
Pourquoi est-ce qu'ils font cela ?

Where did he find my bag ? ➔ Où a-t-il trouvé mon sac ?
Où est-ce qu'il a trouvé mon sac ?

When did you get up ? ➔ Quand vous êtes-vous levé ?
Quand est-ce que vous vous êtes levé ?

Complex inversion will again be necessary in cases like these when the subject is a noun rather than a pronoun.

For example: How did the thief find the jewels ?
- → How, the thief, did he find the jewels ?
- → Comment le voleur a-t-il trouvé les bijoux ?

or : Comment est-ce que le voleur a trouvé les bijoux ?

Why was your husband looking out the window ?
- → Why, your husband, was he looking out the window ?
- → Pourquoi votre mari regardait-il par la fenêtre ?

or : Pourquoi est-ce que votre mari regardait par la fenêtre ?

OTHER USES OF INVERSION

* Verbs of speech or thought must be inverted when they follow immediately after *direct speech*, i.e. immediately after the end of the inverted commas.

  For example: M. Leblanc a dit "Salut !" → "Salut !" a dit M. Leblanc.

  Les filles ont crié "Au revoir". → "Au revoir" ont crié les filles.

  Il a hurlé "Au secours !" → "Au secours !" a-t-il hurlé.

  Nous avons dit "Bonjour". → "Bonjour" avons-nous dit.

It is important to note that the order of words is slightly different for a verb in the passé composé, depending on whether the subject of the verb is a noun or a pronoun. With a noun, (e.g. the first two examples above) the two parts of the verb stay together and follow directly after the inverted commas. With a pronoun, (e.g. the last two examples) the pronoun and the auxiliary verb are inverted and the past participle comes at the end.

It is also important to pay attention to the word order in the case of reflexive verbs.

For example: "The soup is cold", they complained. (**se plaindre**)
- → "La soupe est froide", se sont-ils plaints.

"When will they arrive ?" I wondered. (**se demander**)
- → "Quand est-ce qu'ils arriveront ?" me suis-je demandé.

NB Because these examples of inversion are not questions, it is of course not possible to use an *est-ce que* construction as an alternative. This is one reason why you should try to master the word order in cases of inversion right through this lesson.

* Appendix I on p.121 gives examples of two other situations where inversion may occur, but a knowledge of these is not required for the purposes of the following exercise.

— EXERCISE —

Translate the following sentences, applying the various rules for the formation of questions and for inversion. Try to translate all the questions in two different ways, using *est-ce que* and *inversion*.

(1) "Did you close the door ?" she asked.
(2) "Yes, didn't you hear the noise ?" I answered.   (le bruit)
(3) Does the bus go as far as Nice ?
(4) "Did she sit down on this chair ?" John asked.
(5) "I don't know," his sister answered.
(6) Why are they going to bed so early ?   (se coucher)
(7) Why did they go to bed so early last night ?
(8) "When will I be famous ?" the singer asked.
(9) "I'm tired," he told his wife.
(10) "Me too," she admitted.
(11) "Did we buy enough food ?" the girls wondered.   (la nourriture)
                                                      (se demander)
(12) Did the girls buy enough food ?
(13) "Help !" the man shouted.
(14) "Aren't you spending too much money ?" they asked.   (dépenser)
(15) Didn't he study French last year ?
(16) Didn't he dress himself very quickly ?
(17) Is your sister washing her hair again ?
(18) Didn't she wash her hair yesterday ?

LESSON 11

USE OF *DEPUIS* AND SIMILAR CONSTRUCTIONS

We have already seen that when using *venir de* and *si*, care must be taken as regards the choice of tense in French. In Lesson 8 also, there were several examples of situations where the tense required in French was different from what we would have expected in English. This lesson deals with another case in which French tense usage has a different logic from the English equivalent, namely the use of *depuis* (for, since) to express an event in progress, whether at the present time or at some moment in past time.

> To tell how long something **has been** happening (which means that it still **is** happening in the present), use the **Present Tense** + *depuis*.
>
> To tell how long something **had been** happening (which means that it still **was** happening at some point in the past) use the **Imperfect Tense** + *depuis*.

For example: Depuis combien de temps attendez-vous ?
(How long **have** you been waiting ?)
J'attends depuis vingt minutes.
(I **have been** waiting for twenty minutes.)

   Present tense because the waiting carries on into the present

   Depuis combien de temps attendiez-vous quand elle est arrivée ?
   (How long **had** you been waiting when she arrived ?)
   J'attendais depuis vingt minutes.
   (I **had been** waiting for twenty minutes.)

Imperfect tense : the waiting was carrying on at a point in the past

   Nous **habitons** ici depuis ma naissance.
   (We have been living here since I was born.)
   Nous **habitions** ici depuis dix ans quand nous avons décidé de déménager.
   (We had been living here for ten years when we decided to move.)

As alternatives to *depuis* in order to convey the idea of a continuing event,

$\begin{bmatrix} Voici \\ Voilà \\ Il\ y\ a \\ Cela\ fait \end{bmatrix}$ + amount of time + *que* + verb in present tense

are used to tell what *has been* happening (and still is).

– 45 –

Similarly, ⎡Il y avait⎤ + amount of time + *que* + verb in imperfect tense
          ⎣Cela faisait⎦

are used to tell what *had been* happening (and still was).

For example: ⎡Voici⎤
             │Voilà│ longtemps que j'étudie cette leçon.
             │Il y a│
             ⎣Cela fait⎦

= J'étudie cette leçon *depuis* longtemps.   (I've been studying this lesson for ages.)

⎡Il y avait⎤   deux mois qu'elle venait à notre école quand elle est tombée malade.
⎣Cela faisait⎦

= Elle venait à notre école *depuis* deux mois quand elle est tombée malade.
  (She had been attending our school for two months when she became sick.)

In all of these sentences so far, some event is **still in progress** either in the present or in the past. It is possible, however, to use *depuis* with the passé composé or the pluperfect for a **completed event** leading up to some point in present or past.

For example: Il a écrit plusieurs romans depuis deux ans.
               (He has written several novels in the past two years.)

               Il m'a dit à Noël qu'il avait écrit plusieurs romans depuis deux ans.
               (He told me at Christmas that he had written several novels in the previous two years.)

   Compare: Il écrit des romans depuis deux ans.
                (He has been writing novels for two years.) i.e. he is still doing so.
       and: Il écrivait des romans depuis deux ans, quand il a eu son accident.
                (He had been writing novels for two years when he had his accident.)

As a general rule, any **negative** sentence with *depuis* cannot be regarded as expressing an event still in progress, and so one would expect to use passé composé or pluperfect, rather than present or imperfect.

For example: Je n'ai pas mangé de bonbons depuis une semaine.
               (I haven't eaten any sweets for a week.)

               Il s'est rendu compte qu'il n'avait rencontré personne depuis midi.
               (He realised that he hadn't met anybody since noon.)

When the word **since** (expressing the idea of time) introduces a verb, i.e. when it acts as a conjunction rather than a preposition, it is translated by *depuis que*. Once again the choice of tense depends on whether the event is considered as continuing or completed.

For example: Depuis que j'étudie la grammaire {mon français s'améliore.   (continuing)
                                                {mon français s'est amélioré. (completed)

   (Since I have been studying grammar, {my French has been improving.)
                                         {my French has improved.)

              Depuis que nous avons déménagé, {je me fais beaucoup d'amis.   (continuing)
                                                {je me suis fait beaucoup d'amis. (completed)

   (Since we moved house, {I have been making lots of friends.)
                            {I have made lots of friends.)

NB See Lesson 23 p.93 for use of *pendant* and *pour* to translate **for** + a period of time.

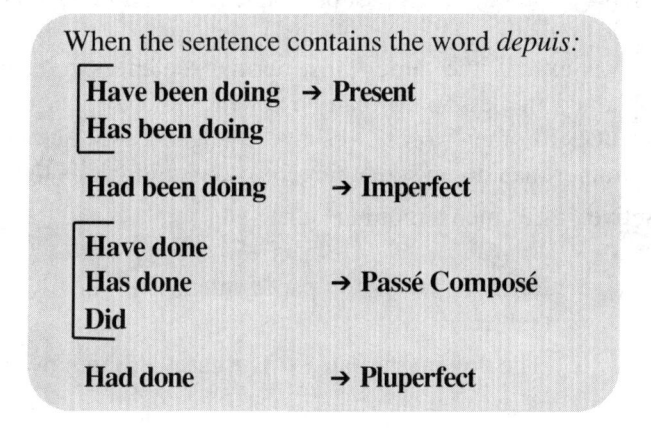

When the sentence contains the word *depuis*:

[Have been doing
Has been doing] → Present

Had been doing → Imperfect

[Have done
Has done
Did] → Passé Composé

Had done → Pluperfect

— EXERCISE —

Translate the following sentences.

(1) He has been on holidays for three weeks.
(2) He had been on holidays for three weeks when his wife died.
(3) We had been walking for two hours when we saw the castle.
(4) We have been walking for two hours and I'm tired.
(5) I have been working hard since they gave me the tools. (les outils)
(6) She said that I hadn't met her sister since 1985.
(7) How long have they been doing their homework ?
(8) They haven't done any homework since Friday.
(9) You had been reading for half an hour when the dog started barking. (aboyer)
(10) I have been reading for the past twenty minutes.
(11) She has read the whole book since yesterday morning.
(12) Since I left school, I haven't seen either John or Catherine.

LESSON 12

PASSIVE VOICE
USE OF *ON*

In Lesson 2, we saw that every tense in English has an equivalent in the Passive Voice, where the subject is not acting but being acted upon.

> For example: **Active Voice**   **Passive Voice**
> I hate   I am hated
> She injured   She was injured
> They will thank   They will be thanked

Each of these three examples of a verb in the passive voice consists of some tense of the verb "to be" (I am, she was, they will be) plus a past participle (hated, injured, thanked).

The structure in French is exactly the same. Most normal sentences containing subject, verb and direct object (explained in Lesson 16) can be rewritten so that the object becomes the subject of a new sentence. In other words, we have changed from Active Voice to Passive Voice, and the subject, rather than doing something, has something done to him / her / it.

For example: (a)   Active   : Le chien a mordu le chat.
                                              (object)
                    Passive : Le chat a été mordu par le chien.
                                  (subject)
                    (The dog bit the cat. → The cat was bitten by the dog.)

(b)   Active   : L'assassin a tué plusieurs femmes.
                                     (object)
       Passive : Plusieurs femmes ont été tuées par l'assassin.
                       (subject)
       (The murderer killed several women.
                  → Several women were killed by the murderer.)

(c)   Active   : Paul aime Pauline.
                              (object)
       Passive : Pauline est aimée de Paul.
                    (subject)
       (Paul loves Pauline. → Pauline is loved by Paul.)

Each of these examples consists of some tense of *être* (**a** and **b** passé composé; **c** present) plus a past participle.

The past participle always agrees with the subject of the passive sentence, but the **été** of the passé composé contained in the passive can never agree.

For example: Lucie a été remerci*e*.
　　　　　　Pierre et Lucie ont été remerci*és*.
　　　　　　Lucie et Françoise ont été remerci*ées*.

Any of the tenses available in French may be used in the passive voice.

For example: Des ouvriers *sont* renvoyés par le patron chaque année.
　　　　　　(Some workers are sacked by the boss every year.)
　　　　　　Des ouvriers *ont été* renvoyés par le patron jeudi dernier.
　　　　　　(Some workers were sacked by the boss last Thursday.)
　　　　　　D'autres ouvriers *avaient été* renvoyés par le patron la semaine précédente.
　　　　　　(Other workers had been sacked by the boss the week before.)
　　　　　　Des ouvriers *étaient* renvoyés chaque année pendant mon enfance.
　　　　　　(Some workers were sacked every year when I was a child.)
　　　　　　Des ouvriers *seront* renvoyés par le patron la semaine prochaine.
　　　　　　(Some workers will be sacked by the boss next week.)
　　　　　　Des ouvriers *seraient* renvoyés par le patron s'il le fallait.
　　　　　　(Some workers would be sacked by the boss if necessary.)
　　　　　　Des ouvriers *auraient été* renvoyés par le patron, s'ils n'avaient pas accepté sa décision.
　　　　　　(Some workers would have been sacked by the boss if they hadn't accepted his decision.)

It is important to watch out for verbs in the passive voice when telling a story in French : she was seen, they were taken to hospital, he was wounded, and so on. Be careful in particular not to confuse passives with the imperfect tense : she was seeing him every evening, they were taking their time, etc.

USE OF *ON*

The Passive Voice is not used quite as often in French as in English. The most common way of avoiding it is to use *on* (= somebody / people in general / all of us) and a verb in the Active Voice. The use of *on* implies that the action is carried out by a human agent and that it is intentional, but it is not stated who exactly carries out the action.

For example: All the windows have been opened. → On a ouvert toutes les fenêtres.
　　　　　　The furniture was dusted yesterday. → On a épousseté les meubles hier.
　　　　　　French is spoken in Geneva. → On parle français à Genève.

Appendix H (p.120) gives examples of the use of reflexive verbs to translate the English passive. This construction is not necessary for the purposes of the exercise which follows this lesson.

The indirect object of a verb (explained in Lesson 16) cannot become the subject of a passive in French.

Take for example the sentence : 'They gave me the message', where 'the message' is the direct object and 'me' (= to me) the indirect object. It is possible to translate "The message was given to me" directly into French as "Le message m'a été donné", but there is no direct French equivalent for "I was given the message." To translate this, one has to use *on* + active voice, i.e. "On m'a donné le message".

Similarly the sentence "We told him the story", where 'the story' is the direct object and him (= to him) the indirect object, can be rewritten in French as "The story was told to him" (L'histoire lui a été racontée.), but not as "He was told the story". The translation of that would be : "On lui a raconté l'histoire."

Other examples of phrases for which there is no direct French equivalent include : **she was offered** a new job, **you were shown** the painting, **they were asked** several questions.

To spot the difficulty, tell yourself that **she** was not being offered, it was the job that was being offered; **they** were not being asked, it was the questions that were being asked; etc.

— EXERCISE —

Translate the following sentences, giving two different translations wherever possible.

Remember that **on + active voice** cannot be used if the English sentence reveals who did the action (e.g. The food was cooked **by John**.). On the other hand, a literal translation into the passive is not possible whenever an indirect object has been used as a subject in English (e.g. I was given some. He was told).

(1) They were punished by their father. (punir)
(2) The room will be cleaned tomorrow morning. (nettoyer)
(3) She was forgotten because of the accident.
(4) She was told that she was wrong.
(5) The solution to the problem has not yet been found.
(6) I was asked if I wanted to leave.
(7) The bananas will be sold before six o'clock.
(8) The letter was signed by three witnesses. (un témoin)
(9) You would be given a prize if you finished that.
(10) The book that I sold yesterday had been bought by my brother three years ago.
(11) The young girls were woken by their mother. (réveiller)
(12) He was answered very quickly.

LESSON 13

PRESENT PARTICIPLE
INFINITIVE IN FRENCH WHERE ENGLISH HAS PARTICIPLE
PERFECT INFINITIVE AFTER *APRÈS*

PRESENT PARTICIPLE

The part of the verb which ends in -ing in English is called the present participle. It is formed in French by taking the 1st person plural of the present tense (the *nous* part) and replacing the *-ons* by *-ant*.

For example: acheter → nous achetons → **achetant**
  choisir → nous choisissons → **choisissant**
  boire → nous buvons → **buvant**
  faire → nous faisons → **faisant**

There are only three exceptions :

Être → *étant*; Avoir → *ayant*; Savoir → *sachant*.

(a) If the present participle is used as an adjective, it agrees with the noun it describes.

  For example: une soucoupe volante   de l'eau courante.
    (a flying saucer)   (running water)

(b) When used as a verb, the present participle does not agree.

  For example: La femme conduisant la camionnette m'a salué.
    (The woman driving the van waved at me.)

(c) Following *en*, this part of the verb is called the *gerund*.
  It translates "**while** doing something" or "**by** doing something" and again there is no agreement.
  For example: en mangeant (while eating, by eating)
    Elle a répondu en riant. (Laughing, she answered.)
    En cherchant sa cravate, il a trouvé l'argent qu'il avait perdu.
    (While looking for his tie, he found the money he had lost.)

NB (i) En + present participle can only be used when the gerund and the main verb in the sentence have the same subject.

  For example it could not be used for a sentence like "While **he** was looking for his tie, I found the money." That type of sentence would be translated by *pendant que* + imperfect : Pendant qu'il cherchait sa cravate, j'ai trouvé l'argent.

(ii) Consequently, the inclusion of *en* can alter the meaning.

"Je l'ai rencontré entrant dans le bâtiment." means that I met him when **he** was entering the building.

"Je l'ai rencontré en entrant dans le bâtiment." means that I met him when **I** was entering the building.

INFINITIVE IN FRENCH WHERE ENGLISH HAS PARTICIPLE

In many places where English has a present participle in -ing, French uses an **infinitive** instead.

- After verbs of seeing, hearing and the other senses

    For example: Il a vu son père tomber de l'échelle.
    (He saw his father **falling** from the ladder.)
    Ils entendaient les enfants jouer et chanter.
    (They could hear the children **playing** and **singing**.)

    The infinitive may be placed immediately after the main verb.
    For example: J'ai entendu chanter les oiseaux. (I heard the birds singing.)

- The notion of being occupied at something is expressed by *à + infinitive* where English has a present participle :

    For example: J'ai passé la matinée *à peindre*.
    (I spent the morning painting.)
    Elle était assise *à regarder* les passants.
    (She was sitting watching the passers-by.)

- After any other preposition apart from **en** :

    without knowing it → sans le *savoir*
    instead of laughing → au lieu de *rire*
    before going out → avant de *sortir*
    for reading → pour *lire*

In some cases where the infinitive expresses a completed action, the ordinary infinitive is replaced by a combination of the auxiliary verb and the past participle. This combination, known as the *Perfect Infinitive*, is most common after *après* : instead of saying "after doing something", French says "after having done something".

So in practice, use *après avoir + past participle* to translate "after doing something" if the verb is conjugated with avoir :

For example: Après avoir acheté des fruits, Jean a mangé une pomme.
Après avoir travaillé pendant une heure, nous nous sommes reposés.

For être verbs, use *après être + past participle* :

For example: Après être rentrée chez elle, Marie a téléphoné à ses parents.
Après être montés au deuxième étage, ils ont sonné à la porte.

(**NB** agreement of the past participle with the subject for être verbs.)

For reflexive verbs, use *après + reflexive pronoun + être + past participle* :

For example: Après s'être déshabillée, elle s'est couchée.
Après m'être reposé, je me suis remis au travail.
Après nous être levés de bonne heure, nous étions un peu fatigués.

Just like *en* + present participle in the first section of this lesson, this construction can only be used when the two parts of the sentence have the same subject. For example, it could not be used to translate a sentence like : After **she** finished with the book, **I** started to read it. (The most obvious way to translate that would be to use *après que* followed by a past tense. You will be reminded of this distinction on p.58.)

Here are some more examples of the use of the perfect infinitive, following prepositions other than *après*. In each case, the reason it is used is that the action is presented as something completed :

Thank you for **sending** me a postcard. → Merci de m'*avoir envoyé* une carte postale.

He was punished for **breaking** a window. → Il a été puni pour *avoir cassé* une fenêtre.

She left the exam hall without even **trying** to answer one question. → Elle a quitté la salle d'examen sans même *avoir essayé* de répondre à une seule question.

Thank you for **coming** to see me. → Je vous remercie d'*être venu* me rendre visite.

— EXERCISE —

Translate the following sentences.

(1) After coming out of the house, we saw the boys playing football.
(2) He ate an apple while reading the paper.
(3) He brushed his teeth after reading the paper. (se brosser les dents)
(4) After brushing his teeth, he spent the afternoon writing letters.
(5) Without trying to listen, I soon heard the women chatting.
(6) Thanks for telling me all the news.
(7) By studying like that, you will learn lots of French.
(8) After reading for ten minutes, we spent an hour swimming.
(9) While she washed her hair, I watched the builders working.
(10) While she washed her hair, she thought about her boyfriend.

LESSON 14

THE SUBJUNCTIVE MOOD
VERBAL CONSTRUCTIONS FOLLOWED BY SUBJUNCTIVE

The *indicative mood* (which includes all the normal present, past and future tenses already studied) presents an idea as a 'fact', whether that fact exists in the present, past or future. The *subjunctive mood* is not used for definite facts, but instead it presents a verb as a 'hypothetical idea', for example as something dependent on an emotion or a wish. Because the subjunctive has almost died out completely in English, it is easier just to study the situations where it is used in French, rather than worry about its exact meaning.

There are four tenses in the subjunctive in French, but the imperfect and pluperfect are rarely used. (Examples are given in Appendix J, p. 123.)

FORMATION OF PRESENT SUBJUNCTIVE

For all verbs, whether regular or irregular, except the ten listed at the bottom of this page and the top of the next, the present subjunctive is derived from the **third person plural of the present tense**. Replace the *-ent* with the endings : *-e, -es, -e, -ions, -iez, -ent*.

For example : **Finir** : *finissent* : finisse, finisses, finisse, finissions, finissiez, finissent.
               Vendre : *vendent* : vende, vendes, vende, vendions, vendiez, vendent.
               Dire : *disent* : dise, dises, dise, disions, disiez, disent.

Complication :

Any irregular verb whose present tense has a change of stem for the *nous* and *vous* parts, will also have a change of stem for the *nous* and *vous* parts in the subjunctive. When this happens, the 1st and 2nd plural are exactly the same as the 1st and 2nd plural of the **imperfect tense**, while the other four parts follow the basic rule above and get their stem from the 3rd plural of the present tense.

For example: **Devoir** : *doivent* : doive, doives, doive, devions, deviez, doivent.
               Venir : *viennent* : vienne, viennes, vienne, venions, veniez, viennent.

This will occur with verbs such as boire, croire, prendre, recevoir, voir.

IRREGULAR PRESENT SUBJUNCTIVES

Être : je sois, tu sois, il soit, nous soyons, vous soyez, ils soient.
Avoir : j'aie, tu aies, il ait, nous ayons, vous ayez, ils aient.

Faire : je fasse, etc. (no change in stem in plural)
Pouvoir : je puisse, etc. (no change in stem in plural)
Savoir : je sache, etc. (no change in stem in plural)

Aller : j'aille, etc. (with change in stem - nous *allions*, vous *alliez*)
Vouloir : je veuille, etc. (with change in stem - nous *voulions*, vous *vouliez*)
Valoir : je vaille, etc. (with change in stem - nous *valions*, vous *valiez*)

Falloir : il faille
Pleuvoir: il pleuve

FORMATION OF PERFECT SUBJUNCTIVE

Just as the perfect indicative (passé composé) consists of two parts, the present indicative of *avoir* or *être* and the past participle, so the perfect subjunctive is also a compound tense, consisting of the *present subjunctive of avoir or être* and the *past participle*.

Perfect Subjunctive of **Donner** :	Perfect Subjunctive of **Aller** :
j'aie donné	je sois allé(e)
tu aies donné	tu sois allé(e)
il ait donné	il soit allé
elle ait donné	elle soit allée
nous ayons donné	nous soyons allé(e)s
vous ayez donné	vous soyez allé(e)(s)
ils aient donné	ils soient allés
elles aient donné	elles soient allées

Conduire (1st person plural)   : nous ayons conduit.
Se Dépêcher (3rd person plural) : elles se soient dépêchées.

USES OF THE SUBJUNCTIVE

Standing alone

The subjunctive only stands alone to express a prayer, a wish or a command in the 3rd person :
Que Dieu vous *bénisse* ! (God bless you.) *Vive* la république ! (Long live the Republic !)
Qu'il *parte* ! (Let him be off !) Que tout le monde *comprenne* ! (Let everyone understand !)

In a subordinate clause

The subjunctive follows either a particular type of verb in the main part of the sentence, or a particular conjunction, or a particular type of relative pronoun construction.

The remainder of this section deals with the several types of verb which are followed by the subjunctive.

(i) **Verbs expressing Emotion**

including : avoir peur que, craindre que, regretter que, s'étonner que, aimer que, être surpris / désolé / content / ravi / bouleversé que, se plaindre que.

For example: Je suis surpris qu'elle *vienne*. (I'm surprised that she's coming.)

Je m'étonne qu'elle *soit venue*. (I'm amazed that she came.)

Nous sommes désolés que *tu te sois cassé* la jambe.
(We are very sorry that you broke your leg.)

(ii) **Verbs expressing Command**

including : souhaiter que, préférer que, désirer que, conseiller que, ordonner que, demander que, vouloir que, exiger que, défendre que, interdire que.

For example: Nous préférons que vous *restiez* avec nous. (We prefer you to stay with us.)

Tu veux qu'il te *rende* visite ? (Do you want him to visit you ?)

(iii) **Verbs expressing Lack of Knowledge**

i.e. verbs of denial (such as douter, nier, ignorer) used **positively** and verbs of opinion / belief (such as croire, dire, penser, espérer, être sûr) used in the **negative** or as a **question**.

For example: Je doute qu'ils *soient descendus*. (I doubt whether they went downstairs.)

Il ne pense pas que les étudiants *veuillent* partir.

(He doesn't think the students want to leave.)

but Il pense que les étudiants *veulent* partir.

Croyez-vous que le président *ait* tort ? (Do you believe the president is wrong?)

but Je crois que le président *a* tort.

Hence *je crois que, je pense que* and *j'espère que* are **not** followed by the subjunctive.
(In fact, the last is usually followed by the future.)

(iv) **Impersonal Verbs** (i.e. verbs whose subject is always **Il**, meaning *it*)

A subjunctive is required after phrases such as : il faut que, il est temps que, il est juste que, il n'est pas certain que, il se peut que, il est possible que, il est impossible / fâcheux / regrettable que, il vaut mieux que, etc.

For example: Il faut qu'elle *sache* la vérité. (It's necessary for her to know the truth.)

Il est possible qu'ils *soient* déjà *arrivés*. (It's possible they've already arrived.)

Some impersonal verbs that present a verb as a fact are not followed by the subjunctive, e.g. il est certain / évident que, il est probable que, il *me* semble que (it seems to me that), il *lui* semble que (it seems to him / her that).

For example: Il me semble que la partie **est** perdue. (It seems to me that the game is lost.)

NB In all these cases so far, the subjunctive verb in the subordinate clause follows *que* and there are different subjects for the two parts of the sentence. With most of these verbs, an infinitive (or **de** + infinitive) can be used when the two verbs have the same subject :

For example: Je suis ravi *de venir* te voir.   (compare : **Je** suis ravi que **tu** *viennes* me voir.)

               Il est temps *de partir*.   (compare : **Il** est temps que **vous** *partiez*.)

               Vous désirez le *remercier* ?   (compare : **Vous** désirez que **nous** le *remercions* ?)

               Il faut *faire* de son mieux.   (compare : **Il** faut que **tu** *fasses* de ton mieux.)

— EXERCISE —

Translate the following sentences, bearing in mind the rules as to when the subjunctive is required in a subordinate clause.

(1) I'm glad that he's doing the washing-up.
(2) I'm glad that he did the washing-up.
(3) It is impossible for her to know that.
(4) It is certain that she knew that.
(5) She wants us to be able to understand her.
(6) Do you believe that he drinks too much?
(7) Do you believe that he drank too much?
(8) They suggested that you should go to their house. (suggérer)
(9) He's very sad that she doesn't want to marry him.
(10) She doesn't believe I was born in Scotland.
(11) I believe that he is going to forget his books.
(12) I'm afraid they've already gone to bed. (se coucher)
(13) It's a shame that they're selling their car.
(14) We're surprised that they sold their car.

LESSON 15

CONJUNCTIONS FOLLOWED BY SUBJUNCTIVE
RELATIVE PRONOUN CONSTRUCTIONS FOLLOWED BY SUBJUNCTIVE

The previous lesson dealt with various types of verb which are followed by a subjunctive. This section deals with the other two types of signal which require the subjunctive.

CONJUNCTIONS

(i) Conjunctions of Time : *Avant que* (before)
Jusqu'à ce que / *En attendant que* (until)

For example: Je vais partir avant qu'il (ne)* me *voie*. (..before he sees me)
Je suis parti avant qu'il (ne)* m'*ait vu*. (..before he saw me)
Il chantera jusqu'à ce qu'on lui *dise* de s'arrêter.
(He will sing until he is told to stop.)

* This *ne* is explained in Appendix G, p.119.

NB 1 : **Before** → *Avant* + noun : avant les vacances, avant midi.

Avant de + infinitive : Il s'est lavé les mains avant de manger.
(used when both verbs refer to the same subject.)

Avant que + subjunctive : as in examples above.
(used when there is a different subject in each part of the sentence)

NB 2 : According to the rules of grammar, **After** should never be followed by a subjunctive, even though this may be heard in colloquial French.

Après + noun : après la rentrée, après la guerre.

Après + perfect infinitive (when subject doesn't change) {See Lesson 13}

Après que + indicative (when subject changes)

For example: Après qu'il s'est assis, nous avons commencé à parler.

(ii) Conjunctions of Purpose : *Pour que* / *Afin que* (in order that)
De peur que / *De crainte que* (for fear that)

For example: Pour que vous *puissiez* m'entendre, je vais parler plus haut.

NB Distinguish between *Pour* / *Afin de* + *infinitive* when the subject does not change, and *Pour que* / *Afin que* + *subjunctive* when the subject changes.

For example: Je fais des économies { afin d'acheter une nouvelle voiture.
{ afin que nous *achetions* une nouvelle voiture.

De sorte que, *De manière que* and *De façon que* (so that/in such a way that) are followed by the subjunctive when they suggest purpose or intention (= in order that) but by the indicative if they mean "with the result that".

For example: On ne lui a pas apporté son petit déjeuner,
        { de façon qu'elle *descende* à la cuisine.   (It was done intentionally.)
        { de façon qu'elle est descendue à la cuisine. (That was the result.)

(iii) Conjunctions of Concession or Reservation :

Bien que / Quoique (although / though / even though),
Pourvu que (provided that), *À condition que* (on condition that),
Sans que (without), *À moins que* (unless).

For example: Ils ont voté pour nous, quoique *nous n'ayons rien fait* pour eux.
        Il ne retournera pas, à moins qu'elle ne* lui *écrive* pour s'excuser.
        Pourvu que l'examen ne *soit* pas difficile, tu auras une bonne note.

* This *ne* is explained in Appendix G, p.119.

NB   **without :** *Sans* + noun (article usually omitted)
             Sans + infinitive (same subject for both verbs)
             Sans que + subjunctive (different subject for 2nd verb)

For example: Il est sorti, sans savoir où il devait aller.
        Il est sorti, sans que nous *sachions* où il allait.
        (He left without our knowing where he was going.)

RELATIVE PRONOUN CONSTRUCTIONS FOLLOWED BY SUBJUNCTIVE

In three cases where the clause introduced by a relative pronoun presents a notion as an unproved personal assessment, the verb should be subjunctive:

(a) when the relative pronoun refers back to a noun accompanied by a superlative adjective (i.e. le plus / la plus + adjective : See p.89) or by any adjective having the force of a superlative (seul, unique, premier, dernier, le moins + adjective, etc).

    For example: C'est le film le plus violent que j'*aie jamais vu*.
                 C'est le seul livre où l'on *puisse* trouver ces renseignements.
                 Voilà le poème le moins intéressant qu'il *ait écrit*.

But if the second clause presents an established fact, there will be no subjunctive.

    For example: C'est la plus grande salle que nous avons dans cette école.

(b) when the relative pronoun follows a negative main clause.

    For example: Il n'y a rien que je *veuille* acheter dans ce magasin.
                 Il n'y a que lui qui *sache* résoudre ce problème.

(c) when the relative pronoun introduces a clause expressing a requirement or a desirable qualification : something whose existence is uncertain.

    For example: J'aimerais avoir un ami qui me *comprenne*.
                 Nous voulons acheter une maison qui *ait* le chauffage central.

<u>But</u> if the situation exists in fact, there will be no subjunctive.

For example: J'ai trouvé un ami qui me comprend.

Nous avons découvert une maison qui a le chauffage central.

SUMMARY OF MAIN USES OF SUBJUNCTIVE :

- when there is a change of subject following :
  - **(i)** verbs expressing Emotion
  - **(ii)** verbs expressing Command
  - **(iii)** verbs expressing Lack of Knowledge
  - **(iv)** Impersonal verbs

- after some conjunctions, particularly :

  Avant que, Jusqu'à ce que,
  Pour que, Afin que, De peur que,
  Bien que, Quoique, Pourvu que,
  Sans que, À moins que

- after a relative pronoun which follows the three types of main clause shown on the previous page

— EXERCISE —

Translate the following sentences, bearing in mind the rules as to when a subjunctive is required in a subordinate clause.

(1) I will work until six, even though I'm very tired.
(2) Unless you tell me your name, I won't be able to help you.
(3) He remained there until she arrived.
(4) There is no subject that takes as much time as French.
(5) She always leaves before I finish my work.
(6) She left yesterday before you finished your work.
(7) Although he drives carefully, he had three accidents last week.
(8) The children wash their hands without my having to tell them to.
   (NB - to have to → devoir
         - to tell them to → "to say it to them")
(9) That's the most intelligent man I know.
(10) I read the most interesting part so that they would want to read the whole book themselves.
(11) She looked at me in such a way as to make me feel ashamed. (avoir honte)
(12) She looked at me in such a way that I felt ashamed.
(13) The little girl obeys her father for fear he would punish her.   (punir)
(14) Until I get his letter, I won't say any more about it.

LESSON 16

DIRECT AND INDIRECT OBJECT PRONOUNS

Most English sentences contain subject, verb and object, in that order.

	SUBJECT	VERB	OBJECT
(a)	The dog	chased	the cat.
(b)	They	chased	us.
(c)	The man	spoke	to his sister.
(d)	He	spoke	to them.

The 'subject' is usually the person or thing doing the action.
The 'object' is the person or thing at the receiving end of the action.

Sentences (a) and (b) have a **Direct Object**, because the object follows directly after the verb, with no preposition in between.

Sentences (c) and (d) have an **Indirect Object**, because there is a preposition (the word **to**) between verb and object.

In sentences (b) and (d) "us" and "them" are *object pronouns* (i.e. words replacing nouns and acting as the object of a verb), the first **direct**, the second **indirect**.

DIRECT OBJECT PRONOUNS

me (m' before vowel) = me   nous = us
te (t' before vowel) = you   vous = you
le (l' before vowel) = him / it   les = them
la (l' before vowel) = her / it

se (s') = himself/herself/itself   se (s') = themselves

They come before the verb of which they are the object :
For example: Je *les* vois. (I see them.)   Il *nous* déteste. (He hates us.)
            Ils *m'*ennuient. (They bore me.)   Je *t'*aime. (I love you.)

If the sentence has two verbs, you must decide to which verb the object belongs.
For example: We're going to buy *them*. → Nous allons *les* acheter.
            I'd like to see *her*. → J'aimerais *la* voir.

In a negative sentence, the object pronoun cannot be separated from the verb, so the *ne* comes after the subject, and the *pas* at the end.

The negative forms of the four sentences on the previous page would be :

    Je ne les vois pas.   Il ne nous déteste pas.
    Ils ne m'ennuient pas.   Je ne t'aime pas.

Similarly for a formal inverted question, whether positive or negative, the object pronoun is always found directly before the verb.

For example: Does he hate us ? → Nous déteste-t-il ?
                Doesn't he hate us ? → Ne nous déteste-t-il pas ?
                Don't we see her ? → Ne la voyons-nous pas ?

In the passé composé (or any other compound tense), the object pronoun goes before the *avoir* part of the verb, and it stays directly in front of the *avoir* part, both in the negative and question forms. (Lesson 20 explains how this may alter the spelling of the past participle.)
For example:

    Je les ai pris. (= I took them.)   Nous l'avons oublié. (= We forgot him.)
    Tu les as pris.   Vous l'avez oublié.
    Il les a pris.   Ils l'ont oublié.
    Elle les a pris.   Elles l'ont oublié.

(Negative)   She didn't hear me.   → Elle ne m'a pas entendu.
                        They didn't frighten you. → Ils ne t'ont pas effrayé.

(Question)   Did she hear me ?   → M'a-t-elle entendu ?
                        Did they frighten you ?   → T'ont-ils effrayé ?

(Negative Question) Didn't she hear me ?   → Ne m'a-t-elle pas entendu ?
                        Didn't they frighten you ? → Ne t'ont-ils pas effrayé ?

NB   If in doubt about word order in a question, there is always the option of using
      est-ce que : Est-ce qu'elle m'a entendu ?
                        Est-ce qu'elle ne m'a pas entendu ?

INDIRECT OBJECT PRONOUNS

Indirect Object Pronouns in French are the same as direct object pronouns for 1st person and 2nd person.

me = me / to me, *te* = you / to you, *nous* = us / to us, *vous* = you / to you.

3rd person singular is *lui* meaning 'to him' or 'to her'.
3rd person plural is *leur* meaning 'to them'.

These indirect object pronouns are used to replace the preposition *à* and a noun referring to a person or people. The rules for their position are the same as for the direct object pronouns.

For example: We are speaking to Anne. → Nous parlons *à Anne*.
We are speaking to her. → Nous *lui* parlons.

He sent a letter to my cousins. → Il a envoyé une lettre *à mes cousins*.
He sent a letter to them. → Il *leur* a envoyé une lettre.

They didn't give the pen to her. → Ils ne *lui* ont pas donné le stylo.

Did you tell the story to him ? → *Lui* as-tu raconté l'histoire ?

SUMMARY

Object Pronoun directly before Verb

Object Pronoun directly before *avoir* in Passé Composé

Him / Her / Them → Le / La / Les

To him / To her / To them → Lui / Leur

DISTINGUISHING BETWEEN DIRECT AND INDIRECT OBJECTS

Care must be taken when using the words him, her and them, to distinguish between *le / la / les* (direct objects) and *lui / leur* (indirect objects). Study the following sentences :

(a) After finding the books, I gave them to John.
(b) He met his cousins and gave them some money.
(c) They sent her home early.
(d) Did you send her a postcard ?

In sentences (a) and (c), the underlined objects are **direct** (*les* and *la*) because the books were the things being given and she was the person being sent. In sentences (b) and (d) the underlined objects are **indirect** (*leur* and *lui*). In (b), the direct object is "some money" (the thing being given) and 'them' means "**to** them". In (d), the direct object is "a postcard" (the thing being sent) and 'her' means "**to** her".

Among the verbs which may take two objects, one direct and one indirect, are :
donner, montrer (to show), envoyer (to send), dire, demander*, rendre (to return, give back) and offrir (to offer).

Other verbs follow a different logic in French and in English :

– Taking a direct object where English demands indirect :
Regarder = to look *at*, **Écouter** = to listen *to*, **Attendre** = to wait *for*, **Demander*** = to ask *for*, **Chercher** = to look *for*, **Payer** = to pay *for*.

– Taking an indirect object where English demands direct :

téléphoner à quelqu'un	→	to phone somebody,
promettre à quelqu'un	→	to promise somebody,
répondre à quelqu'un	→	to answer somebody, to reply **to** somebody
obéir à quelqu'un	→	to obey somebody.
rappeler à quelqu'un	→	to remind somebody.

For example: I'm looking *at him*.	→	Je le regarde. (direct)
We phoned *them*.	→	Nous leur avons téléphoné. (indirect)
Did she send *him* a letter ?	→	Lui a-t-elle envoyé une lettre ? (indirect)
I paid *for it*.	→	Je l'ai payé. (direct)
Are you listening *to her* ?	→	Tu l'écoutes ? (direct)
You didn't answer *them*.	→	Vous ne leur avez pas répondu. (indirect)

* The verb *demander* may require special care. Note the following :

He asked for the book.	→	Il a demandé le livre.
He asked his sister for the book.	→	Il a demandé le livre à sa soeur.
He asked for it.	→	Il l'a demandé.
He asked her to leave.	→	Il lui a demandé de partir.

SUMMARY

Direct Object
- when there is no preposition before object (in French)
- with *Regarder, Écouter, Attendre, Demander, Chercher, Payer*

Indirect Object
- when the French verb is followed by *à*
- in places where the word *to* is understood in English

— EXERCISE A —

Replace the italicised nouns with pronouns.

(1) Je connais *Hélène*.
(2) J'écris souvent à *Hélène*.
(3) J'ai acheté *ce livre*.
(4) Je n'ai pas acheté *ce livre*.
(5) Elle parlait à *ses copains*.
(6) Elle ne parlait pas à *ses copains*.
(7) Nous avons oublié *son prénom*.
(8) Nous n'oublions jamais *les journaux*.
(9) Ils donneront l'argent à *Philippe*.
(10) Ils donneront *l'argent* à Philippe.

— EXERCISE B —

Translate the following, distinguishing carefully between direct and indirect objects.

(1) He told her the story.
(2) We didn't wait for him.
(3) They listened to it.
(4) She chose him yesterday.
(5) We didn't speak to them.
(6) They are losing her.
(7) I never looked at him.
(8) He's phoning us now.
(9) We are choosing them.
(10) You sent her a letter. *
(11) I hear them every day.
(12) She often listens to him.
(13) She gave them the money.
(14) We answered you. *
(15) You showed her the book. *
(16) I don't see them.
(17) They paid for it.
(18) He is forgetting me today.
(19) They looked for him at home.
(20) Are you going to buy them ? *
(21) She offered him the sweets.
(22) Did you phone her yesterday ? *

* tu and vous forms

LESSON 17

RELATIVE PRONOUNS

A relative pronoun is a word replacing a noun (definition of any pronoun) which joins two short sentences together to form one longer sentence.

The two most common relative pronouns are *qui* and *que*, used to translate 'who', 'which', 'that' or 'whom' in English. If the relative pronoun is replacing the **subject** of one of the two short sentences, *qui* is used, while *que* replaces the **direct object** of one of the sentences. Either pronoun can be used to refer to people or things; the distinction between them depends on the subject / object structure of the sentence.

Que changes to *qu'* when followed by a vowel or h mute, but *qui* never drops its *i*.

Study the following examples :

    (A) *Tu* as trouvé *le billet*.   **(B)** *Le billet* était sur la table.
       (subject)   (object)   (subject)   (object)

These sentences may be combined in two different ways. If we say : "Tu as trouvé le billet, (which) était sur la table.", sentence (A) has been retained in full and the relative pronoun (which) replaces the subject of sentence (B), therefore we use the subject pronoun *qui*.

On the other hand, if we say : "Le billet, (which) tu as trouvé, était sur la table.", this time sentence (B) has been retained in full and the object of sentence (A) is missing, therefore we use the object pronoun *que*.

* Tu as trouvé le billet, *qui* était sur la table.
* Le billet, *que* tu as trouvé, était sur la table.

    (C) *Le fermier* porte *un gros sac*.   **(D)** *Nous* regardons *le fermier*.
       (subject)   (object)   (subject)   (object)

Again, there are two ways to combine these sentences. If we say : "Le fermier, (whom) nous regardons, porte un gros sac.", sentence (C) has been retained in full and the object of sentence (D) is missing, therefore we use the object pronoun *que*.

But if we say : "Nous regardons le fermier, (who) porte un gros sac.", sentence (D) has been retained in full and the relative pronoun (who) replaces the subject of sentence (C), therefore we use the subject pronoun *qui*.

* Le fermier, *que* nous regardons, porte un gros sac.
* Nous regardons le fermier, *qui* porte un gros sac.

NB The relative pronoun is often left out in English, and when this happens, *qui* must never be used to translate into French.

    For example: The car (which) he was driving had no insurance.
                Is she going to eat the food (that) he cooked ?

As a rule of thumb for deciding whether to use *qui* or *que* in any particular case, you can follow this procedure :

(1) Put in as many commas as possible to divide the sentence into its parts. (This will help you to see what the two original separate sentences were.)
(2) See if the verb in the section of the sentence which begins with the relative pronoun has a subject.
(3) If the verb has no subject, use the subject pronoun → *qui*.
(4) If the verb already has a subject, use the object pronoun → *que*.

Preposition + Relative Pronoun

The following examples have a relative pronoun following a preposition:

The girl *with whom* you're going out. → La fille {*avec qui*   tu sors.
                                               {*avec laquelle*

The stick *with which* he hit us. → Le bâton *avec lequel* il nous a frappés.

The men *on whom* you are counting. → Les hommes {*sur qui*   tu comptes.
                                                 {*sur lesquels*

The tables *on which* I put the cups. → Les tables *sur lesquelles* j'ai mis les tasses.

Hence:
For people : either **Preposition + Qui** (not used after *entre* or *parmi*)
          or   **Preposition + Lequel**.

For things :   **Preposition + Lequel**.

Depending on which word it refers to, lequel agrees : *le*quel, *la*quelle, *les*quels, *les*quelles.

Be careful when *à* or *de* combine with *lequel* :

    à :   auquel (masc. sing.),   à laquelle (fem. sing.),
          auxquels (masc. pl.),   auxquelles (fem. pl.).

    de: duquel (masc. sing.),   de laquelle (fem. sing.),
          desquels (masc. pl.),   desquelles (fem. pl.).

The boy to whom I'm speaking. → Le garçon auquel je parle. (*or* à qui)
The boys to whom I'm speaking. → Les garçons auxquels je parle. (*or* à qui)
The house of which he was speaking. → La maison de laquelle il parlait.
The women of whom he was speaking. → Les femmes desquelles il parlait. (*or* de qui)

Dont (whose, of which, of whom)

Dont is a relative pronoun containing the preposition *de*. It can be used to replace *de qui*, or any form of *duquel, de laquelle*. This means that it could have been used in the last two examples.

If you study the following examples, you will note that whenever *dont* is used, it is the first word in the clause (i.e. in that part of the sentence), and it must be followed by a subject and then a verb.

(a) Je te présente Mireille. Tu as déjà rencontré le frère **de Mireille**.
→ Je te présente Mireille, *dont* tu as déjà rencontré le frère.
(This is Mireille, whose brother you've already met.)
[of whom you've already met the brother]

(b) L'ouvrier a emporté le marteau. J'ai besoin **du marteau**.
→ L'ouvrier a emporté le marteau, *dont* j'ai besoin.
(The worker has taken away the hammer that I need.)
[of which I have need]

(c) Je connais une fille. Un des frères **de cette fille** est champion olympique.
→ Je connais une fille, *dont* un des frères est champion olympique.
(I know a girl, one of whose brothers is an Olympic champion.)
[of whom one of the brothers]

The *de* which is the reason for the use of *dont* may indicate possession (as in examples **a** and **c** above), or it may be linked to a verb like avoir besoin *de* (example **b**), se plaindre *de*, se moquer *de*, etc.

Où

Où can function as a relative pronoun of place, translating:
where, to which, in which, at which.

For example: La ville où il habitait...   L'hôtel où je l'ai rencontré...

Où must also be used to translate 'when' in phrases such as :

Le soir où il est arrivé...   (The evening that he arrived...)
Le matin où il a plu...   (The morning when it rained...)
Le jour où ils reviendront... (The day they will return...)

Ce qui / Ce que

The basic meaning of these pronouns is **what** (literally : that which), in phrases such as :

Il m'a raconté *ce qu*'il avait vu. (He told me what he had seen.)
Je sais bien *ce qui* les intéresse. (I know well what interests them.)
Elle a mangé *ce que* tu as mis dans le frigo. (She's eaten what you put in the fridge.)
Après *ce qui* vient d'arriver, je me méfie de toi. (After what has happened, I don't trust you.)

The choice as to whether *ce qui* or *ce que* should be used depends on whether the verb following needs a subject or object, similar to the choice between *qui* and *que* on pp. 66 and 67.

After *tout, ce* must be inserted before the relative pronoun to translate "all that" or "everything that".
For example: Je ferai *tout ce qui* sera possible et *tout ce que* vous voudrez.
(I'll do all that is possible and all that you want.)

Either *ce qui* or *ce que* is also used when the relative pronoun refers not to one particular noun, but to a whole clause, i.e. to one particular section of the sentence.
For example: Nous venons d'acheter une nouvelle voiture { qui nous plaît.
{ ce qui nous plaît.

(In the first case, we like the new car; in the
second, we like the idea of owning a new car.)

Elle a refusé, ce que j'ai trouvé étonnant de sa part.

(She refused, which I found surprising.)

NB The word *what* at the start of a question will not be translated by *ce* + relative pronoun, just as *whose* introducing a question is not translated by *dont*.

SUMMARY

- *Qui / Que* (= who, which, that, whom)
  choice depends on the verb following :

  Qui when verb following needs a subject
  Que when verb following already has a subject

- *Preposition + relative pronoun* → prep. + *qui* (for people)
  prep. + *lequel* (for things)

- *Dont* (= whose, of which, of whom)
  used whenever the noun being replaced followed *de*

- *Où* (= where, to which, in which, when)

- *Ce qui / Ce que* (= what) choice depends on the verb following

— EXERCISE A —

Translate the following sentences, using either *qui* or *que / qu'* in each case.

(1) We gave her the bag you had found.
(2) We gave her the bag that has a big hole near the bottom.
                                            (un trou)   (le fond)
(3) This is the man who taught me French in school.
(4) This is the man that I met yesterday.
(5) The book she is reading isn't very interesting.
(6) Did you get the newspaper I sent you ?
(7) The girl who arrived at nine is still there.
(8) The girl who has just gone out is called Lucy.

— EXERCISE B —

Translate the following sentences, giving careful thought to the choice of relative pronoun in each case.

(1) We know a boy whose parents live in London.
(2) What you did yesterday is not important.
(3) What happened yesterday is not important. (to happen : se passer)
(4) I lost the key that we open the door with.   (NB : rephrase sentence first)
(5) I've never met the men to whom she sent it.
(6) She was wearing a blue dress the morning she left home.
(7) This is the man about whom I complained. (to complain : se plaindre de)
(8) They have everything they want.
(9) They have everything they need.   (to need : avoir besoin de)
(10) The lady for whom I bought the present is my aunt.

LESSON 18

STRESSED PRONOUNS
OTHER PRONOUN OBJECTS : Y AND EN
POSITION AND ORDER OF OBJECT PRONOUNS

STRESSED PRONOUNS

The stressed pronouns can be recognised as the pronouns used following prepositions like avec, sans, derrière, après, à cause de, contre, and especially **chez** :

chez *moi*, chez *toi*, chez *lui*, chez *elle*, (+ chez *soi* : impersonal, used with *on*)
chez *nous*, chez *vous*, chez *eux*, chez *elles*.

Other uses of stressed pronouns include :

(a) following *c'est* and *ce sont*
For example: Est-ce que c'est toi ? C'est lui qui l'a fait.

(b) when the pronoun stands alone, for example in answer to a question
For example: Qui a cassé la fenêtre ? - Lui ! Eux ! Elle !

(c) following *que* in comparisons, or in the *ne + que* construction
For example: Jean court plus vite que toi.   Elle n'aime que lui.
Elle est plus forte que lui.   Il n'y a que moi.

(d) in combination with *même(s)* :
For example: lui-même (himself), elle-même (herself), soi-même (oneself),
eux-mêmes / elles-mêmes (themselves)

(e) with another pronoun for emphasis
For example: Moi, je suis intelligent. Il n'est pas d'accord, lui.

(f) in composite subjects
For example: Lui et moi, nous travaillons bien ensemble.
Toi et ta soeur, vous êtes très jolies.

(g) with *à* to indicate possession
For example: La valise noire est à moi.
Ce chien n'est pas à lui.

Y AND EN

Both *Y* and *En* are object pronouns. As such, they precede the verb and in a compound tense (e.g. passé composé) they precede the auxiliary verb.

The most common meaning of *y* is 'there' (in that place, to that place).
For example: J'y vais souvent. (I often go there.)
           Nous y sommes arrivés très tard. (We arrived there very late.)
           Je n'y vais jamais. (I never go there.)

It is also used with verbs which take the preposition **à** before an object, to replace both the preposition and a pronoun such as 'it' or 'them'. (Some of these verbs are listed in Lesson 23, p.95.)

For example: s'intéresser à : Je m'intéresse au sport. (I'm interested in sport.)
                            Je m'y intéresse. (I'm interested in it.)
          penser à : Nous pensons à l'examen. (We're thinking about the exam.)
                   Nous y pensons. (We're thinking about it.)

→ **Y** = à + it / them

The most common meanings of *en* are 'of it', 'of them', 'some', 'any,'
For example: Il en a beaucoup. (He has a lot of it / them.)
           Elle n'en a pas.   (She hasn't any.)
           Combien de frères avez-vous? J'en ai deux. (I have two.)

It is also used following verbs which take the preposition **de** before an object, to replace both the preposition and a pronoun such as 'it' or 'them'. (Some of these verbs are listed in Lesson 23, p.96.)

For example: se moquer de : Il s'est moqué de mes chaussures. (He laughed at my shoes.)
                             Il s'en est moqué. (He laughed at them.)
        avoir besoin de : Tu as besoin de ce livre. (You need this book.)
                        Tu en as besoin. (You need it.)

→ **En** = de + it / them

Because *Y* and *En* are not used very often to refer to people, one can draw a distinction between the pronouns used to refer to *people* and *things*, following verbs taking **à** and verbs taking **de** .

Verb + **à**
- \+ person → either *lui* or *leur*
- \+ things → *y*

Verb + **de**
- \+ person → *de* + stressed pronoun
- \+ things → *en*

Study the following examples :

(a) Ressembler à :

Elle ressemble à son père.	(She looks like her father)
Elle *lui* ressemble.	(She looks like him.)
Ta jupe ressemble à la mienne.	(Your skirt looks like my one.)
Ta jupe *y* ressemble.	(Your skirt looks like it.)

(b) Obéir à :

Ils obéissent aux profs.	(They obey the teachers.)
Ils *leur* obéissent.	(They obey them.)
Nous avons obéi aux règles.	(We obeyed the rules.)
Nous *y* avons obéi.	(We obeyed them.)

(c) Se souvenir de :

Je me souviens de ma grand-mère.	(I remember my grandmother.)
Je me souviens d'*elle*.	(I remember her.)
Vous souvenez-vous de ce jour-là ?	(Do you remember that day ?)
Vous *en* souvenez-vous ?	(Do you remember it ?)

(d) Se servir de :

Je me suis servi de mes amis.	(I used my friends.)
Je me suis servi d'*eux*.	(I used them.)
Il se sert de son couteau.	(He's using his knife.)
Il s'*en* sert.	(He's using it.)

NB With just a few verbs such as penser à, faire attention à and se fier à (to trust, rely on), the ordinary indirect object pronouns (me, te, lui, etc.) are not used, and instead one finds à + the stressed pronoun. (p.71)

For example: Je pense à elle. (I'm thinking of her.)
Faites attention à moi. (Pay attention to me.)

(This last construction is not necessary for the purposes of the exercise which follows this lesson.)

POSITION AND ORDER OF OBJECT PRONOUNS

(i) In all situations except for positive commands (i.e. for all statements, questions and commands in the negative), the object pronouns are placed before the verb, in the following order :

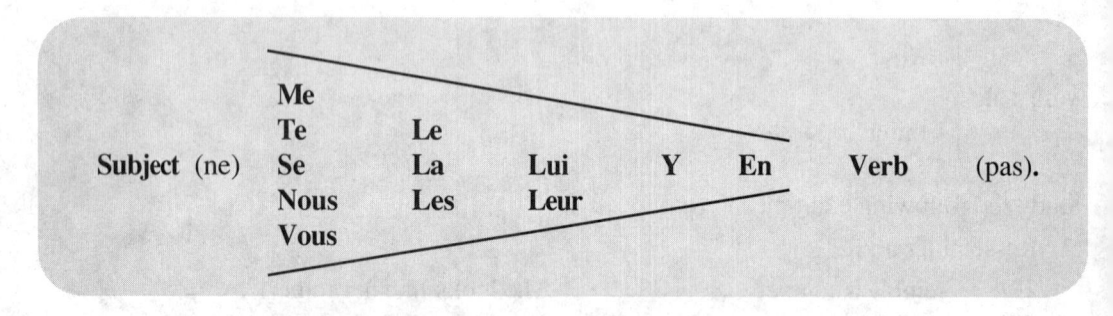

| Subject | (ne) | Me
Te
Se
Nous
Vous | Le
La
Les | Lui
Leur | Y | En | Verb | (pas). |

For example: Il ne *nous les* donnera pas. (He won't give them to us.)

Elle va *m'en* offrir trois. (She's going to offer me three [of them].)

Vous ne *nous les* envoyez jamais. (You never send them to us.)

Ils ne *t'y* rencontrent pas. (They don't meet you there.)

In a compound tense, like the passé composé, the pronouns follow exactly the same order, coming directly before the auxiliary verb :

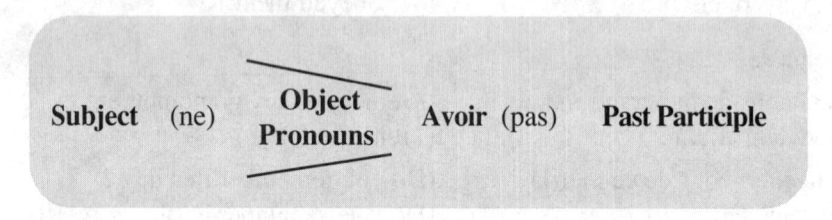

| Subject | (ne) | Object Pronouns | Avoir | (pas) | Past Participle |

For example: Il ne *nous l'*a pas présenté. (He didn't introduce him to us.)

Nous *le lui* avons envoyé. (We sent it to her.)

Est-ce que tu *me l'*as donné ? (Did you give it to me ?)

Je ne *leur en* ai pas montré beaucoup. (I didn't show them much of it.)

(ii) For positive commands : - the pronouns follow the verb.
- they come in the same order as in English.
- they are linked by hyphens.
- me → *moi*; te → *toi*.

This means that positive and negative commands have a different order for the pronouns :

For example: (a) Donnez-*les-nous*.   Ne *nous les* donnez pas.
                    (Give them to us.)   (Don't give them to us.)
               (b) Envoyez-*la-moi*.   Ne *me l'* envoyez pas.
                    (Send her to me.)   (Don't send her to me.)
               (c) Prends-*le*.   Ne *le* prends pas.
                    (Take it.)   (Don't take it.)
               (d) Lève-*toi*.   Ne *te* lève pas.
                    (Get up.)   (Don't get up.)

NB Object pronouns always precede *voici* and *voilà*.
For example: *Me* voici. (Here I am.)
              La voilà (There she is.)

— EXERCISE —

Translate the following sentences, paying particular attention to the pronouns :

(1) I offered it to them yesterday.
(2) I didn't offer it to you.
(3) Put them on the table.
(4) Don't put them on the table.
(5) The question was difficult but I answered it.
(6) She didn't answer it.
(7) Answer it now.
(8) Don't answer it.
(9) It is they who use the camera. (se servir de)
(10) We didn't use it.
(11) Give it to them.
(12) Don't give it to them.
(13) I met those people but I don't remember them. (se souvenir de)
(14) I read those books but I don't remember them.
(15) They invited me to a wedding at their house.
(16) My husband didn't like them and I didn't attend it because of him. (assister à)

LESSON 19

AGREEMENT AND POSITION OF ADJECTIVES
POSSESSIVE ADJECTIVES

REGULAR AGREEMENT OF ADJECTIVES

An adjective is a descriptive word used to qualify a noun. The noun to which the adjective applies may be masculine or feminine, singular or plural, and the ending of the adjective changes in order to agree with its noun. It takes -e if the noun is feminine and -s if plural.

For example: Le livre est petit.   La maison est petit*e*.

Les jardins sont petit*s*.   Les fenêtres sont petit*es*.

If the adjective already ends in -*e*, the masculine and feminine forms are the same :
un chapeau rouge   une chemise rouge

If the adjective ends in -*s* or -*x*, the masculine singular and masculine plural are the same :
un pantalon gris   des pantalons gris.

IRREGULAR AGREEMENT OF ADJECTIVES

Adjectives ending in	change to	Example
-é -er -x -f	-ée -ère -se -ve	carré → carrée premier → première précieux → précieuse neuf → neuve
-el } -en } -et * } -as } -on } -eil }	Double the final consonant and add -e	naturel → naturelle canadien → canadienne muet → muette bas → basse bon → bonne pareil → pareille

* except for the following four :   secret → secrète   discret → discrète
inquiet → inquiète   complet → complète

faux → fausse (false)   ⎡ blanc → blanche (white)
favori → favorite (favourite) ⎢ franc → franche (frank)
frais → fraîche (cool, fresh) ⎣ sec → sèche (dry)
long → longue (long)

– 76 –

doux	→ douce	(sweet, soft)	⎡fou	→ folle	(mad)
roux	→ rousse	(red-haired)	⎣mou	→ molle	(soft)
malin	→ maligne	(shrewd)			
sot	→ sotte	(foolish)	⎡public	→ publique	(public)
gros	→ grosse	(large, fat)	grec	→ grecque	(Greek)
gentil	→ gentille	(kind)	⎣turc	→ turque	(Turkish)
épais	→ épaisse	(thick)			
bref	→ brève	(short)	⎡aigu	→ aiguë	(sharp)
			⎣contigu	→ contiguë	(adjoining)

Adjectives whose masculine singular ends in *-eau* (e.g. beau, nouveau) end in *-eaux* in the masculine plural.

For example: les beaux quartiers

Most adjectives whose masculine singular ends in *-al* (e.g. marginal, national, original, terminal) end in *-aux* in the masculine plural.

For example: les parlements nationaux

There are just a few adjectives with a special form which is used if the adjective agrees with a noun which is (1) masculine, (2) singular, (3) beginning with vowel / h mute.

       beau → belle ..... bel (nice, beautiful)
       nouveau → nouvelle ..... nouvel (new)
       vieux → vieille ..... vieil (old)

This means that these particular adjectives have **five** forms, instead of the usual four :
le nouveau livre, le nouvel an, la nouvelle voiture,
les nouveaux livres / ans, les nouvelles voitures.

Similarly, the demonstrative adjective – This / That / These / Those – has a special form if the noun is masculine, singular and begins with a vowel or h mute :

This / That → ⎡ Ce   before masculine, singular, consonant
                | Cette   before feminine, singular
                ⎣ Cet   before masculine, singular, vowel / h mute

These / Those → Ces   before all plurals.

For example: ce garçon, ce livre, ce pays, cette femme, cette valise, cette école, cette boîte,
              cet homme, cet appartement, cet animal, ces boîtes, ces animaux.

If one particularly wants to distinguish between 'this' and 'that', or between 'these' and 'those', one can add *-ci* to the noun (for this / these) and *-là* (for that / those).

For example: ce livre-ci   (this book here)
             cet appartement-là (that particular flat)
            ces maisons-ci   (these houses)
            ces maisons-là   (those houses)

Another irregular adjective is the word 'all' :

tout	(masculine singular)	→	tout le monde*, tout le bâtiment
toute	(feminine singular)	→	toute la ville, toute la maison
tous	(masculine plural)	→	tous les hommes, tous les vêtements
toutes	(feminine plural)	→	toutes les filles, toutes les fois

*Always followed by verb in singular.

For example: Tout le monde est arrivé sain et sauf.

The word *demi* (half) does not agree **in front of** a noun.

For example: une demi-heure but trois heures et demie.

The same applies to the word *nu* (naked, bare).

For example: Il est sorti nu-tête / (la) tête nue.
　　　　　　　Elle a marché nu-pieds / (les) pieds nus.

Compound adjectives of colour (e.g. pale yellow) do not agree at all.

For example: une robe vert foncé (a dark green dress)
　　　　　　　des yeux bleu clair (light blue eyes).

The same applies to most *nouns* used as adjectives of colour, including words such as *orange*, *cerise* (cherry-coloured), *crème* (cream-coloured) and *marron* (chestnut-coloured).

For example: des oeillets crème (cream-coloured carnations)
　　　　　　　des rubans orange (orange ribbons).

NB   Ordinary adjectives of colour such as *blanc, bleu, brun, gris, jaune, noir, rouge, vert*, etc. show normal agreement with the noun. This also applies to the noun *rose* (= pink) when used as an adjective.

POSITION OF ADJECTIVES

Most adjectives usually follow the noun, including all adjectives of colour and nationality :
　　a green car　　　　　　→ une voiture verte
　　a shy, frightened girl → une fille timide et effrayée.

The following rhyme gives a list of those common adjectives, which, like *autre* and the ordinal numbers (premier, deuxième, troisième, etc.) usually **precede** the noun :

> Mauvais, Méchant, Vilain, Beau,
> Petit, Haut, Vieux, Joli, Gros,
> Nouveau, Gentil, Jeune et Bon,
> Grand et Meilleur, Vaste ct Long.

Sometimes the meaning of an adjective is determined by its position :

(a)	un ancien élève	(former)	un chateau ancien	(very old)
(b)	une pauvre fille	(pitiable)	un pays pauvre	(without money)
(c)	ma propre famille	(own)	une pièce propre	(clean)
(d)	une chère amie	(beloved)	un cadeau cher	(expensive)
(e)	le dernier métro	(last in a series)	la semaine dernière	(just passed)
(f)	un grand homme	(big, great)	un homme grand	(tall)
(g)	le même jour	(same)	le jour même	(very)

POSSESSIVE ADJECTIVES

The words 'my' sister, 'his' mother, 'their' cousin are descriptive words and, just like any other adjective, must agree with the noun to which they are attached.

My → *Mon* before all masculine singular nouns and before all feminine singular nouns beginning with a vowel or h mute.
Ma before all feminine singular nouns beginning with a consonant.
Mes before all plural nouns.

Similarly Your → *Ton* for masculine singular (and feminine singular with vowel).
Ta for feminine singular with consonant.
Tes for all plurals.

In the third person singular, there is no distinction in French between **his** and **her**. The choice of possessive adjective depends on the gender of the noun. Because "mère" is feminine, **his** mother → *sa* mère (which could also translate "her mother"). Because "père" is masculine, **her** father → *son* père (which could also translate "his father").

Ses is used when either **his** or **her** is followed by a plural.

Our → *Notre* (singular) and *Nos* (plural)
Your → *Votre* (singular) and *Vos* (plural)
Their → *Leur* (singular) and *Leurs* (plural)

My	:	mon frère	ma soeur	mes parents
Your	:	ton frère	ta soeur	tes parents
His	:	*son* frère	*sa* soeur	*ses* parents
Her	:	*son* frère	*sa* soeur	*ses* parents
Our	:	notre frère	notre soeur	nos parents
Your	:	votre frère	votre soeur	vos parents
Their	:	leur frère	leur soeur	*leurs* parents

NB (i) Be very careful with the choice of adjective to translate his / her
→ determined by gender of noun.

(ii) **Ses** means either *his* or *her*, but never *their*.

(iii) ma / ta / sa can never be used before a vowel.

(iv) *m'* never occurs meaning 'my'.
t' and *s'* are not possessive adjectives either.

(v) Don't mix up leur / leurs (their) with the plural pronoun *leur*
(= to them : indirect object)

(vi) *à lui* and *à elle* may be added to the noun to provide a clear distinction between his and her : sa mère à lui = his mother
sa mère à elle = her mother.

— EXERCISE —

Translate the following phrases.

(1) His first sister.
(2) Her new uncle.
(3) Her new uncles.
(4) His own mother.
(5) Her favourite brother.
(6) His present wife. (actuel)
(7) His red-haired sisters.
(8) My beautiful apartment.
(9) This apartment.
(10) This beautiful apartment.
(11) These national flags. (un drapeau)
(12) These orange flags.
(13) All my daughters.
(14) All my sons.
(15) It's an old idea. (une idée)
(16) It's my idea.
(17) It's her turn. (un tour)
(18) It's your turn. (using the *tu* form)
(19) It's your shadow (using the *tu* form) (une ombre)
(20) An old uncle.
(21) An old aunt.
(22) This old uncle.
(23) This old aunt.
(24) This uncle.
(25) These aunts.
(26) Their original idea.
(27) Their original plans.
(28) These dry clothes.
(29) These dry shirts.
(30) All the grey hats.
(31) All the grey shoes. (une chaussure)
(32) His good ideas.
(33) Her good friends.

LESSON 20

PAST PARTICIPLE AGREEMENT

In any compound tense (passé composé, pluperfect, etc.) the past participle agrees as follows :

(a)   The *être* verbs listed in Lesson 4, p. 18 always agree with the subject.

For example: elle est tombé*e*   nous étions retourné*s*   elles sont né*es*

(b)   All verbs conjugated with *avoir* and all *reflexive verbs* (which are conjugated with être) will agree only if there is a **direct object preceding the verb**.

Look at these examples, in each of which the direct object is underlined. Only when it precedes the verb does the past participle agree.

(a) J'ai vu tes photos.   → direct object *following*
                                 → no agreement of past participle

(b) Tes photos ? Oui, je les ai vues.   → direct object *preceding*
                                             → agreement of past participle

(c) Marie s'est lavé les mains.   → direct object *following*
                                     → no agreement of past participle

(d) Marie s'est lavée.   → direct object *preceding*
                          → agreement of past participle

So whenever you use a compound tense of an avoir verb or a reflexive verb, you must check to see if the sentence contains a direct object preceding (DOP), if you want to know whether the past participle agrees or not.

In all of these cases, you can discover whether a DOP exists by asking the question :

What* did the person involved (verb) ?

Question (a) : What did I see ?   Answer : your photos.
Question (b) : What did I see ?   Answer : them, i.e. photos.
Question (c) : What did she wash ?   Answer : her hands.
Question (d) : What did she wash ?   Answer : herself.

(* strictly speaking "What, or whom, did the person involved (verb) ?")

– 81 –

There are only **five** types of word that may function as a DOP:

(i) The 3rd person direct object pronouns: *le* (him, it), *la* (her, it), *les* (them).
{See Lesson 16, p. 61}

For example: J'ai nettoyé *la fenêtre* et puis je *l'*ai ouverte.

Connaissez-vous *ces garçons* ? Non, je ne *les* ai jamais rencontrés.

(ii) *Me, te, se, nous, vous, se.* (provided they act as direct object)

For example: "Il *m'*a écoutée attentivement," a dit Jeanne.

Il est neuf heures et vous ne *vous* êtes pas encore habillés.

(iii) The relative pronoun *que*. {See Lesson 17, p. 66}

For example: Voici *le livre que* j'ai écrit.   C'est *elle que* tu as vue.

Voilà *les livres qu'*elle a écrits.   Ce sont *elles que* j'ai vues.

(iv) Any noun preceded by *combien de* (how many)

For example: *Combien de maisons* ont-ils construites ? (How many houses did they build ?)

Combien d'hommes a-t-elle tués ?   (How many men did she kill ?)

(v) Any noun preceded by the interrogative word *quel / quelle / quels /quelles* meaning "What — ?" or "Which — ?"

For example: *Quels vêtements* avez-vous achetés dans les soldes ? (What clothes did you buy in the sales ?)

Quelle robe a-t-elle portée ? (Which dress did she wear ?)

Remember, in order to find out whether there is a direct object preceding, ask the question:
"**What** did the person involved (verb) ?":

For example: (in no. iv) What did they build ?   Answer: houses.
                    What did she kill ?   Answer: men.

Because the logic which determines whether an object is direct or indirect is sometimes different in French and in English (as seen in Lesson 16) great care will sometimes be required to decide whether the past participle agrees, when the possible DOP is one of the pronouns from no. (ii) on the previous page, i.e. *me, te, se, nous, vous, se*. If these words precede the verb as an indirect object, there will be no agreement. Consider the following examples, some of which show agreement, some of which do not :

(1) They phoned one another. → Ils se sont téléphoné.
  No Agreement, because the construction *téléphoner à* makes the *se* an indirect object.

(2) She waited an hour for us. → Elle nous a attendus pendant une heure.
  Agreement, because *attendre* takes a direct object, therefore *nous* is a DOP

(3) She got married to the postman. → Elle s'est mariée avec le facteur.
  Agreement, because the literal meaning is "She married 'herself' off to him."

(4) We had already offered you the money. → Nous vous avions déjà offert l'argent.
  No Agreement, because *l'argent* is the direct object, *vous* the indirect.

(5) The sisters wrote each other many letters. → Les soeurs se sont écrit beaucoup de lettres.
  No Agreement, because *se* is indirect, meaning "to each other".

(6) She answered us, saying that she had burnt her finger. → Elle nous a répondu, en disant qu'elle s'était brûlé le doigt.
  No Agreement, because neither the *nous* nor the *s'* is a direct object; *répondre à* takes an indirect object and *le doigt* is the direct object of the verb *brûler*, but following it.

For reflexive verbs which are followed by a preposition [e.g. *s'attendre à* (to expect) and *se passer de* (to do without)] and reflexive verbs whose reflexive pronoun cannot be translated literally [e.g. *s'évanouir* (to faint) and *s'écrier* (to cry out)] the past participle agrees automatically with the reflexive pronoun as if the latter were a direct object.

For example: Ils se sont passés de nourriture pendant une semaine.
  "Au secours !" s'est-elle écriée.

When the *après avoir + past participle* construction (Lesson 13) includes a direct object, this provides a DOP for the past participle, which agrees.

For example: after finding them → après *les* avoir trouvés
  after kissing her → après *l'* avoir embrassée

— EXERCISE —

Examine the following sentences and decide how many of the past participles should show feminine or plural agreement.

(1) Elle s'est bless*é* dans l'accident. (She was hurt in the accident.)

(2) Elle s'est bless*é* les jambes dans l'accident. (She hurt her legs in the accident.)

(3) "Il nous a téléphon*é* mais il ne nous a pas bien écout*é*," ont expliqu*é* les filles. (He phoned us but he didn't listen to us properly," the girls explained.)

(4) "Combien de livres avez-vous achet*é* quand vous êtes entr*é* dans la librairie ?" a demand*é* l'agent à Caroline. ("How many books did you buy when you went into the bookshop?" the policeman asked Caroline.)

(5) Après lui avoir pos*é* cette question, lui et son copain sont part*i*. (After asking her that question, he and his friend left.)

(6) Ils se sont intéress*é* à cette chanson. (They became interested in this song.)

(7) Les garçons, que Marie avait rencontr*é* dans la rue, ont cass*é* une fenêtre ; puis ils se sont échapp*é* en courant, mais quelqu'un les a suiv*i* et a racont*é* toute l'histoire à la police. (The boys, whom Mary had met in the street, broke a window; then they ran off [literally : they escaped by running], but somebody followed them and told the whole story to the police.)

(8) Mon frère et mes deux soeurs sont rest*é* à la maison. (My brother and my two sisters stayed at home.)

(9) "Vous ne nous avez pas donn*é* assez de ces belles fleurs," a di*t* Anne. ("You didn't give us enough of these lovely flowers," said Anne.)

(10) Quelle raison ont-ils donn*é* ? (What reason did they give ?)

(11) Cet homme et sa femme n'ont jamais fai*t* la vaisselle ensemble. (That man and his wife have never done the washing-up together.)

(12) Ils ne se sont jamais parl*é* avec tendresse. (They have never spoken to each other affectionately.)

(13) En fait, ils ne se sont jamais aim*é*. (In fact, they never loved each other.)

(14) Selon les garçons, les bonnes notes qu'ils ont obten*u* à l'examen les ont content*é*, parce qu'ils ne s'y étaient pas attend*u* du tout. (According to the boys, the good marks they got in the exam satisfied them, because they hadn't expected them at all.)

(15) "Il m'a regard*é* comme s'il me détestait," a admi*s* Jeanne. ("He looked at me as though he hated me," Joan admitted.)

LESSON 21

THE ARTICLE

(A) Indefinite Article : un, une, des. (See p. 8, point 8)

> The indefinite article may not be omitted in the plural, as in English.

For example: There were chairs in the room. → Il y avait *des* chaises dans la pièce.
I saw flowers in the garden. → J'ai vu *des* fleurs dans le jardin.

> The indefinite article is not used before a noun which denotes occupation, nationality or religion.

For example: Son père est médecin.   Elle travaille comme secrétaire.
Elles sont Allemandes.   Il est catholique.

NB (i) The indefinite article **will** be used when the noun is accompanied by an adjective.
For example: Son père est *un* médecin bien connu.
C'est *un* bon catholique.

(ii) Adjectives of nationality are not spelt with a capital letter in French unless they apply to people, i.e. unless they are being used as nouns :
une vieille chanson *a*llemande   Nous apprenons l'*a*llemand.
J'ai rencontré quelques *A*llemands pendant mes vacances.

(B) Definite Article : le, la, l', les.

> The definite article is used before nouns used in a general sense and before abstract nouns.

For example: J'aime *les* chevaux.
Il déteste *le* café.
La peur est difficile à surmonter.

So there is a distinction between: *Des* (= some particular examples) and
Les (= all the things in general).

For example: *Les* langues étrangères m'ennuient. (all / in general)
J'ai étudié *des* langues étrangères. (some / a certain number)

J'aime bien *les* émissions au sujet de la nature.
Pendant l'hiver, on a regardé *des* émissions au sujet de la nature.

> The definite article is frequently used with parts of the body
> (instead of the possessive adjective).

For example: Ouvrez *la* bouche.   Il se lave *les* mains.

But the possessive adjective is used when the part of the body is the subject of the verb or when it is accompanied by another adjective.

For example: Mon dos me fait mal.
　　　　　　 Ses yeux sont bleus.
　　　　　　 Il a levé son bras blessé.

Preposition **à** + definite article :　à + le → *au*
　　　　　　　　　　　　　　　　　　　à + les → *aux*

For example: le bureau → Allez au bureau.　　la banque → Allez à la banque.
　　　　　　 l'hôpital → Allez à l'hôpital.　 les magasins → Allez aux magasins.

Hence à le and à les are not possible when *le* and *les* mean **the**.

But they may occur if these words are pronouns, i.e. if *le* = him / it and *les* = them.

For example: J'apprends à le faire.　　→ I'm learning how to make it.
　　　　　　 Je commence à les oublier. → I'm beginning to forget them.

Preposition **de** + definite article :　de + le → *du*
　　　　　　　　　　　　　　　　　　　de + les → *des*

For example: les vêtements *du* garçon　/ *de la* fille
　　　　　　　　　　　　　 de l' homme / *des* femmes.

Again de le and de les are not possible if *le* and *les* mean **the**.

But they may occur if *le* and *les* are pronouns, i.e. if *le* = him / it and *les* = them.

For example: Elle essaie de le trouver.　→ She's trying to find it.
　　　　　　 Refusez-vous de les voir ? → Are you refusing to see them ?

(C) Partitive Article : du, de la, de l', des. (same as de + definite article)

For example: J'ai mangé *du* pain / *de la* viande / *des* oeufs.
　　　　　　 Elle a *du* respect / *de la* haine / *de l'* amitié pour moi.

Three situations where du / de la / des (partitive article) and des (plural of indefinite article) are replaced by **de** :

(1) following the negative.

For example: J'ai des copains. → Je n'ai pas *de* copains.
Je bois souvent du lait. → Je ne bois jamais *de* lait.

(2) following an expression of quantity, such as :

beaucoup de (a lot of, many)   assez de (enough of)
trop de (too much, too many)   plus de (more of)
tant de (so much, so many)   moins de (less of)
autant de (as much, as many)   peu de (not much, not many)
combien de (how much, how many)   **un** peu de (a little)

For example: J'ai des copains. → J'ai autant *de* copains que lui.
Ils ont acheté du pain. → Ils ont acheté un kilo *de* pain.

(3) when a plural adjective precedes the noun.

For example: J'ai des copains. → J'ai *de* bons copains.
J'ai vu des peintures. → J'ai vu *de* belles peintures.

— EXERCISE —

Translate the following sentences :

(1) Tea and coffee are not good for one's health.
(2) Too much coffee is bad for one's health.
(3) He sang French songs at my birthday party.
(4) I like French songs very much.
(5) He burnt his hand while lighting the fire.
(6) His hand is still sore.
(7) There are no books in your bag.
(8) Many students hate exams.
(9) Many of the students I know don't read enough books.
(10) She is a nurse.
(11) We bought ham and eggs in the shop.
(12) We didn't buy any bread.
(13) There are often good films on Channel Four.
(14) They never drink wine.
(15) Wine is quite expensive in Ireland.
(16) I saw children playing in the garden.
(17) She was looking for new clothes for the summer.
(18) She already has as many clothes as her mother.
(19) English people are very polite.
(20) I stayed with English people when I was in China.
(21) He wants to become a lawyer.
(22) I cut my finger with the knife.

LESSON 22

FORMATION OF ADVERBS
COMPARATIVE AND SUPERLATIVE OF ADJECTIVES AND ADVERBS

FORMATION OF ADVERBS

Just as an adjective is a word which describes a noun, an **adverb** tells you more about the action of a verb. In English, most adverbs are formed by adding -ly to an adjective (careful → carefully, greedy → greedily).

In French, adverbs are formed by adding *-ment* to the feminine form of the adjective.
For example: heureux (happy) → heureuse (f) → heureusement (happily)
naturel (natural) → naturelle (f) → naturellement (naturally).

Once an adverb has been formed, it is completely invariable (i.e. it does not agree with any other word by becoming feminine or plural). It is usually placed *after* the verb it qualifies, or it may occur at the beginning of the sentence.

If the masculine form of the adjective ends in a vowel, the *-ment* is added directly to the masculine form, e.g. poli → poliment
vrai → vraiment.
The only exception to this is *gai*, which becomes either gaiement or gaîment.

When the adjective ends in *-ant* or *-ent*, the adverb is formed by changing *-ant* to *-amment* and *-ent* to *-emment*, e.g. récent → récemment (recently)
constant → constamment (constantly).
The exception to this is lent → lentement (slowly) which follows the main rule.

Some adverbs change the final *-e* to *-é* in the formation of the adverb.

For example:
énorme	→ énormément	(enormously)
précis	→ précisément	(precisely)
aveugle	→ aveuglément	(blindly)
profond	→ profondément	(deeply)
commode	→ commodément	(conveniently)
immense	→ immensément	(immensely)
confus	→ confusément	(in a confused way)

Irregular Adverbs :
bon	→ bien	(well)
mauvais	→ mal	(badly)
gentil	→ gentiment	(nicely)
bref	→ brièvement	(briefly)

– 88 –

The adjective *rapide* (quick) has two adverbs : *rapidement* and *vite*, both of which mean "quickly". Because *vite* is an adverb and not an adjective, it is not possible to add -ment to it.

A few French adjectives are used as adverbs. Like all other adverbs, they are invariable (i.e. they do not become feminine or plural).

For example: travailler *dur*   (to work hard)
               parler *bas*   (to speak quietly)
               parler *haut*   (to speak loudly)
               crier *fort*   (to shout loudly)
               coûter *cher*   (to cost a lot)
               refuser *net*   (to refuse point blank)
               tenir *bon*   (to hold firm)
               sentir *mauvais*   (to smell bad)
               aller *droit*   (to go straight)
               chanter *faux*   (to sing out of tune)
               viser *juste*   (to aim accurately)
               couper *court* aux arguments de quelqu'un (to interrupt, cut in on somebody)

COMPARATIVE AND SUPERLATIVE OF ADJECTIVES

Where English adds -er and -est to adjectives in order to compare nouns (e.g. stronger / strongest), French uses the word *plus* (i.e. "more strong" / "the most strong").

For example: Pierre est grand.   Marie est petite.
              Son frère est *plus grand* que lui.   Sa soeur est *plus petite* qu'elle.
              Son cousin est *le plus grand*.   Sa cousine est *la plus petite*.

Adjectives agree fully in the superlative and comparative forms. In the superlative *le plus* changes to *la plus* or *les plus* if the noun is feminine or plural.

Depending on whether the particular adjective is one that precedes the noun (like those listed on p.78) or follows it, the superlative construction le / la / les + plus + adjective may either precede or follow the noun also.

For example: *intelligent* is a normal adjective which follows its noun.
          → C'est un garçon intelligent.
          → C'est *le garçon le plus intelligent* de la classe.
          → Ce sont *les filles les plus intelligentes* de la classe.

But *beau* is one of the common adjectives that usually precedes the noun.
          → C'est une belle fille.
          → C'est *la plus belle fille* de la famille.
          → Ce sont *les plus beaux garçons* de la famille.

[Note the use of *de* rather than *dans* in the above examples.]

The adjective *bon*, being irregular, has *meilleur* (= better) as its comparative form and *le meilleur* (= the best) in the superlative.

For example: Pierre a un *bon* appareil-photo et une *bonne* caméra. François a un *meilleur* appareil-photo et une *meilleure* caméra, mais ceux que je viens d'acheter sont *les meilleurs*.

NB The word *as* is never translated by *comme* in comparisons such as 'as big as', 'not as nice as'.

For example: Cette émission est aussi intéressante **que** l'autre.
(This programme is as interesting as the other one.)

Il n'est pas si bavard **que** son frère.
(He's not as talkative as his brother.)

COMPARATIVE AND SUPERLATIVE OF ADVERBS

Just like adjectives, adverbs also have comparative and superlative forms. Once again the word *plus* is used, but because all adverbs are invariable there is no agreement with the subject and no changing of *le* to *la* or *les*.

For example: Paul travaille soigneusement.   (Paul works carefully.)

Son frère travaille plus soigneusement.   (... more carefully.)

De toute la famille, c'est leur soeur qui
travaille le plus soigneusement.   (... the most carefully.)

The adverb *bien* (= well) is irregular :
Louis nage bien.

Son frère nage *mieux* que lui. (His brother swims better than he does.)

De toute la famille, c'est leur soeur qui nage *le mieux*.
(Of the whole family, their sister swims the best.)

MEILLEUR V. MIEUX

The examples above show that 'better' may be translated by *meilleur* (adjective) or *mieux* (adverb). Similarly 'best' may be translated by **le meilleur / la meilleure** (adjective) or **le mieux** (adverb).

In order to decide whether to use *meilleur* or *mieux*, one must check to see if the word **better** or **best** applies to a noun or a verb :

A is a better swimmer than B. →   Il est meilleur nageur que l'autre.   (adjective with noun)
A swims better than B.   →   Il nage mieux que l'autre.   (adverb with verb)

— EXERCISE A —

Produce adverbs from the following adjectives:

faible	*courageux*	*fréquent*	*absolu*
abondant	*précis*	*mauvais*	*doux*
violent	*lent*	*public*	*premier*
secret	*gentil*		

— EXERCISE B —

Translate the following sentences.
(1) He writes better with his left hand.
(2) These watches are the best because they work the best. (fonctionner)
(3) This is the cleanest room in the house. (propre)
(4) This is the biggest room in the house.
(5) Joan is the friendliest girl in the class.
(6) Joan is the youngest girl in the class.
(7) He works harder than her because she is lazier than him. (paresseux)
(8) Paula runs the fastest of all the girls.
(9) That is the most important question in the exam.
(10) This job suits (convenir) me better than the other one.
(11) My next job will suit me the best of the three.

LESSON 23

PREPOSITIONS

Deciding which preposition to use in various situations is a problem in learning most languages and French is no exception. It is not possible to learn rules telling you when to use a particular preposition; ideally if you are listening to and reading sufficient French on a regular basis, you will gradually learn when to use the various prepositions. The purpose of this lesson is merely to list some of the more basic structures involving prepositions.

- IN

    - in / to a town or city : *à*   e.g. à Paris, à Bordeaux, à Cork.

        NB Towns whose names contain the definite article :
        Le Havre → je vais *au* Havre.   Le Mans → je vais *au* Mans.

    - in / to a country : *en* provided the name of the country is feminine
        (nearly all countries ending in -e)
        e.g. en Irlande, en Allemagne, en Suisse.

        au whenever the name of the country is masculine
        (including all those not ending in -e)
        e.g. au Brésil, au Canada, au Danemark, au Japon, au Liban, au Luxembourg, au Maroc, au Mexique, au Moyen-Orient, au Portugal, au Vatican, au Vietnam, au Zaïre.
        (except if the masculine noun begins with a vowel :
        en Iran, en Irak, en Israël, etc.)

        aux whenever the name of the country is plural
        e.g. aux États-Unis, aux Pays-Bas, aux Antilles.

        NB **from** a country : en → *de / d'*   au → *du*   aux → *des*

    - in this way   : *de* cette façon, *de* cette manière
      in the same way   : *de* la même façon, *de* la même manière
      in a funny way   : *d'*une façon amusante, *d'*une manière amusante
      in the 19th century : *au* dix-neuvième siècle
      in the Middle Ages : *au* moyen âge

    - in + time : *dans*   *for a particular point in time in the future*
            e.g. Nous serons à la maison dans trois minutes.
                Dans deux semaines, les examens commenceront.

        en   *for time within which something is to happen*
            e.g. Il a fait le tour du monde en 80 jours.
                (He went around the world in 80 days.)

- **ON** is usually only translated by *sur* when it means "up on top of"; otherwise *à* is often used instead.

- on television	→ *à* la télé
- on the radio	→ *à* la radio
- on the wall	→ *au* mur
- on the second / third floor	→ *au* deuxième / troisième étage
- on the one hand	→ *d'* un côté
- on the other hand	→ *de* l'autre côté
- on holidays	→ en vacances

- When translating verbs followed by **out of, from,** etc. the French preposition sometimes indicates where the thing is **before** it is touched.

    For example: They drank out of the same glass. → Ils ont bu *dans* le même verre.
    She took it from the shelf. → Elle l'a pris *sur* le rayon.

- **ABOUT** + time : *vers* cinq heures, *vers* midi, *vers* une heure et quart.

    + quantity : *environ* vingt chaises, *environ* cent livres
    or une vingtaine de chaises, une centaine de livres.

    NB to speak about → parler (au sujet) *de* quelque chose
    to think about → penser *à* quelque chose
    (See p.97 for distinction between penser **à** and **de**.)

- **FOR** + periods of time :

    - pour   for intended periods of time in the future
        e.g. L'été prochain, je vais travailler à Londres *pour* deux mois.

    - pendant   for completed periods of time in the past
        e.g. L'été dernier, j'ai travaillé à Londres *pendant* deux mois.

    - depuis   for periods of time up to a point in present or past (as explained in Lesson 11)
        e.g. Je travaille à Londres *depuis* deux mois.
            (I have been working in London for two months now.)

- **WITH** For description *à* is used instead of *avec*.

    For example: a boy with glasses → un garçon à lunettes
    a house with five storeys → une maison à cinq étages
    the lady with the blue hat → la dame au chapeau bleu
    the man with the black hair → l'homme aux cheveux noirs
    the girl with the green eyes → la fille aux yeux verts

- In phrases where English combines a verb describing movement and a preposition giving the direction of the movement, French prefers to let the verb tell the direction of the movement.

  For example: He *ran* **out** of the building. → Il est **sorti** du bâtiment *en courant*.
  She *limped* **across** the room. → Elle a **traversé** la salle *en boîtant*.
  I *jumped* **in**. → Je suis **entré** *d'un bond*.

- Several prepositions in French include the word *de*.

  For example: à côté de (beside),   en dépit de (in spite of),
  le long de (along),   au-dess**us** de (above),
  au-delà de (beyond),   au-dess**ous** de (below),
  en face de (opposite),   près de (near).

  The prepositions *devant* (in front of) and *derrière* (behind) are **not** followed by *de* : devant la voiture, derrière la maison.

  Be careful not to confuse *devant* with **avant**, which means 'before' in terms of time.

- Note the combination of *de* and *en* in the following set phrases :

  de plus *en* plus   (more and more)
  de moins *en* moins   (less and less)
  de temps *en* temps   (from time to time, now and again)
  de jour *en* jour   (from day to day)
  de mal *en* pis   (from bad to worse)
  de long *en* large   (back and forth, to and fro)

Use of à and de with the infinitive or with an object

À and *de* are the two prepositions most frequently used in French. As the following lists show, they follow after certain verbs and are then followed by an infinitive or by an object. None of these lists is meant to be complete. Some of the verbs taking *à* or *de* can be followed by either an infinitive or an object, e.g. *s'attendre à* can mean to expect to do something (infinitive) or to expect something (object). Again *se vanter de* can mean to boast about something (object) or to boast about doing something (infinitive).

We have already been using some of these structures in this course. In Lesson 16, we saw how the indirect objects *lui* and *leur* (referring to people) are used after verbs taking *à*, and in Lesson 18 we saw how *y* and *en* are used to translate 'it' and 'them' (referring to things) after verbs taking *à* and *de* respectively.

Verb + à + infinitive

⎡commencer à	(to begin to,	s'amuser à	(to have fun)
⎣se mettre à	to start to)	apprendre à	(to learn to)
		s'attendre à	(to expect to)
⎡réussir à	(to succeed in,	avoir à	(to have to = *devoir*)
⎢arriver à	to manage to)	chercher à	(to try to = *essayer de*)
⎣parvenir à		consentir à	(to agree to)
		se décider à	(to make up one's mind to,
⎡penser à	(to think of)		to decide reluctantly to)
⎣songer à		s'habituer à	(to get used to)
continuer à **or** de	(to continue to)	hésiter à	(to hesitate to)
		tenir à	(to be anxious to)

Verb + direct object + à + infinitive

aider quelqu'un à	(to help someone to)	
déterminer quelqu'un à	(to convince someone to)	See p.97 for forcer /
encourager quelqu'un à	(to encourage someone to)	obliger quelqu'un à.
habituer quelqu'un à	(to get someone used to)	
inviter quelqu'un à	(to invite someone to)	

Verb + à + object

assister à	(to attend)		nuire à	(to harm)
demander à	(to ask)		plaire à	(to please)
désobéir à	(to disobey)		renoncer à	(to give up)
échapper à	(to escape from)		répondre à	(to answer)
faire mal à	(to hurt)		ressembler à	(to resemble)
se fier à	(to trust)		résister à	(to resist)
s'intéresser à	(to be interested in)		téléphoner à	(to phone)
jouer à	(to play : game)			

Verb + de + infinitive

Most French verbs that can be followed by an infinitive belong to this category, including :

⎡essayer de	(to try to,	s'agir de	(to be a question of)
⎢tâcher de	to attempt to)	{ must always have *Il* (=it) as subject}
⎣tenter de			
		décider de	(to decide to)
⎡cesser de	(to stop)	éviter de	(to avoid)
⎣(s') arrêter de		menacer de	(to threaten to)
		mériter de	(to deserve to)
⎡faire semblant de	(to pretend to)	offrir de	(to offer to)
⎣feindre de		oublier de	(to forget to)
		refuser de	(to refuse to)
		risquer de	(to risk)

Verb + direct object + de + infinitive

accuser quelqu'un de *	(to accuse someone of)
arrêter quelqu'un de	(to stop someone from)
empêcher quelqu'un de	(to prevent someone from)
féliciter quelqu'un de *	(to congratulate someone on / for)
persuader quelqu'un de	(to persuade someone to)
prier quelqu'un de	(to beg someone to)

* normally followed by perfect infinitive, as on p.53
For example: Il a été accusé d'*avoir cambriolé* plusieurs appartements.
(He was accused of having burgled several flats.)

Verb + de + object

s'emparer de	(to catch hold of)	jouer de	(to play : music)
s'apercevoir de	(to notice)	se moquer de	(to make fun of)
s'approcher de	(to approach)	s'occuper de	(to see to)
avoir besoin de	(to need)	se passer de	(to do without)
se charger de	(to undertake)	se plaindre de	(to complain about)
se débarrasser de	(to get rid of)	profiter de	(to take advantage of)
dépendre de	(to depend on)	se servir de	(to use)
se douter de	(to suspect)	se souvenir de	(to remember)
s'échapper de	(to escape from)	se vanter de	(to boast about)

Adjective + à + infinitive

For example:
- bon à manger
- mauvais à boire

- facile à comprendre
- difficile à étudier

prêt à sortir   (ready to go out)
utile à savoir (useful to know)

Adjective + à + noun

For example: nuisible à la santé
(harmful to health)

nécessaire à la santé
(necessary for health)

NB   These adjectives will be followed by *de* in the structure *Il est* + adjective + *de* + infinitive.

For example: Il est difficile d'étudier cette leçon.
Il était nécessaire de leur téléphoner.

Adjective + de + infinitive

Je suis content / fier / heureux / satisfait / surpris / étonné / furieux / fâché / désolé / enchanté / ravi (etc.) d'apprendre cette nouvelle.

Adjective + de + noun

couvert de	(covered with / in)
entouré de	(surrounded by)
jaloux de	(jealous of) etc.

- **Rien / Quelque chose / Quelqu'un** + $\begin{bmatrix} à + \text{infinitive} \\ de + \text{adjective} \end{bmatrix}$

  For example: nothing to do → rien *à* faire

  nothing interesting → rien *d'*intéressant

  something to read → quelque chose *à* lire

  something bad → quelque chose *de* mauvais

  someone to love → quelqu'un *à* aimer

  someone important → quelqu'un *d'*important

- **Repetition of prepositions**

If a preposition in French governs more than one object or more than one infinitive, it must be repeated before each noun and each verb.

For example: She's learning to sing and dance.
→ Elle apprend à chanter et *à* danser.

I was using the hammer and the screwdriver.
→ Je me servais du marteau et *du* tournevis.

- For some verbs, a change of preposition alters the meaning.

Demandez à votre ami *de* partir.		(Ask your friend to go.)
Demandez à votre ami *à* partir.		(Ask your friend if **you** can go.)

penser *à*	: Je pense aux vacances.	(I'm thinking about the holidays.)
penser *de*	: Que pensez-vous de lui ?	(What's your opinion of him ?)

manquer	: Nous avons manqué le train.	(We missed the train.)
manquer *à*	: La mère manque aux garçons.	(The boys miss their mother.)
manquer *de*	: Il manque de courage.	(He lacks courage.)

forcer / obliger quelqu'un **à** faire quelque chose
être forcé / obligé **de** faire quelque chose

For example: Il m'a forcé / obligé *à* les vendre. (He forced me to sell them.)

J'ai été forcé / obligé *de* les vendre. (I was forced to sell them.)

- Verbs such as "to take" or "to borrow" which express the idea of removing something **from** someone require the preposition *à* before the person.

    For example: prendre / enlever (to take away) → Prenez le couteau *aux* enfants.
               arracher (to snatch) → Michel a arraché le journal *à* sa soeur.
               acheter (to buy) → J'ai acheté la ferme *à* mes cousins.
               emprunter (to borrow) → Il veut emprunter de l'argent *à* sa mère.
               cacher (to hide) → Nous *leur* avons caché la vérité.
               voler (to steal) → Le cambrioleur *lui* a volé ses bagues.
                                        (The burglar stole her rings.)

- **Verbs NOT requiring a preposition before an infinitive**

    - pouvoir, vouloir, devoir, falloir (il faut), savoir (knowing how to).

    - aller (to express the immediate future, as explained in Lesson 8).

    - verbs of seeing, hearing, etc. (as explained on p.52)

    - aller and venir (for motion)
        For example: Il est allé chercher son frère.   Venez me voir.

    - croire and espérer (to replace a clause beginning with que)
        For example: Il a cru voir quelqu'un dans le jardin.
                    (He thought he saw someone in the garden.)
                    J'espérais les rencontrer hier.
                    (I hoped I would meet them yesterday.)

    - faire (to get / have something done for you)
        For example: Elle a fait peindre la cuisine.   (She got the kitchen painted.)
                    Il s'est fait couper les cheveux.   (I had my hair cut.)
                  Je me suis fait faire une robe.   (I had a dress made for myself.)

    - many others including :   adorer   oser   (to dare)
                                       aimer   paraître   (to appear)
                                       aimer mieux   (to prefer)   préférer
                                       compter   (to intend to)   prétendre   (to claim to)
                                     désirer   sembler   (to seem)
                                   détester   valoir mieux (to be better)
                                   laisser   (to leave, let)   e.g. Il vaut mieux attendre.
                                                                                       (It's better to wait)

    - faillir (meaning "to come very near to doing something", usually only used in past tense)
        For example: Elle a failli s'évanouir.   (She almost fainted.)
                    J'ai failli manquer le train.   (I almost missed the train.)

- POUR + infinitive

Pour is used in French to express the notion "in order to", "for the purpose of", in places where English often has no preposition before an infinitive. Apart from verbs that are followed by *à* + infinitive (p.95), verbs that are followed by *de* + infinitive (p. 95) and the verbs that can be followed directly by an infinitive (p. 98), other verbs in French will require *pour* before a following infinitive.

For example: Stephen worked hard to earn more money.
→ Étienne a travaillé dur *pour* gagner plus d'argent.

I hired out a lawnmower to mow the lawn.
→ J'ai loué une tondeuse *pour* tondre la pelouse.

— EXERCISE —

Translate the following sentences. This task will require a knowledge of the rules, structures and vocabulary dealt with in Lesson 23.

(1) She ran down[3] to the kitchen.
(2) Last summer, she spent a week in[1] Berlin, he went to[1] Spain and I went to[1] Portugal.
(3) In[1] this way, you will learn[7] to give up[7] your bad habits. (une mauvaise habitude)
(4) He seemed[6] to be looking for something[5] new.
(5) I was hoping[6] to return from[1] Canada from time to time[3], because my brother intends[6] to return from[1] Belgium every month.
(6) We expect[7] to leave about[2] seven and visit about[2] six towns.
(7) That depends[4] on the woman with[2] the long hair.
(8) We were forced[5] to stay there for[2] a month.
(9) Then they forced[5] us to hide the jewels from[6] the police. (les bijoux)
(10) It is easy to[4] boast[4] about one's success, but your success is easy to[4] explain. (son succès)

1 : See p.92.   2 : See p.93.   3 : See p.94.   4 : See p.96.   5 : See p.97.   6 : See p.98
7: See p. 95.

APPENDIX A

IRREGULAR VERBS

As outlined in Lesson 3, in order to be able to use an irregular verb, the parts which you must learn are :

        (1) all of the present tense
        (2) the past participle
        (3) the stem of the future tense

The following list of irregular verbs is set out in order of importance, to encourage you to study and memorise them in a gradual way. Some similar verbs are linked in groups (see symbols to the left of the infinitives).

Many compounds of these verbs are included in the index to irregular verbs on p.105 - 110. For example, if the present tense of *mettre* is "je mets" and the past participle is "mis", then its compound *promettre* will give "je promets" and "promis". Again if *venir* has "ils viennent" (present tense) and "elle viendra" (future), *parvenir* will have "ils parviennent" and "elle parviendra".

NB   All irregular verbs (except *être*) form their **imperfect tense** from the present tense 1st person plural. See p.22.

        All irregular verbs form their **conditional tense** from the stem of the future tense.

        All irregular verbs (except *être, avoir and savoir*) form the **present participle** from the present tense 1st person plural. See p.51.

        Pages 31 and 32 show you how to get the **past historic tense** of all the irregular verbs in this appendix (with the exception of a few verbs like *traire, extraire* and *distraire* which have no past historic).

        Pages 54 and 55 show you how to get the **present subjunctive** of all the irregular verbs in this appendix.

	Present Tense	**Past Part.**	**Future** (1st sing.)
• ÊTRE (to be)	suis, es, est, sommes, êtes, sont	été	*serai*
• AVOIR (to have)	ai, as, a, avons, avez, ont	eu	*aurai*
• ALLER (to go)	vais, vas, va, allons, allez, *vont*	allé	*irai*

– 100 –

	Present Tense	**Past Part.**	**Future** (1st sing.)
• FAIRE (to do, make)	fais, fais, fait, faisons, *faites, font*	fait	ferai
• VOULOIR (to want to)	veux, veux, veut, voulons, voulez, *veulent*	voulu	voudrai
- POUVOIR (to be able to)	peux, peux, peut, pouvons, pouvez, *peuvent*	pu	pourrai
- DEVOIR (to have to)	dois, dois, doit, devons, devez, *doivent*	dû	devrai
• METTRE (to put)	mets, mets, met, mettons, mettez, mettent	mis	mettrai
- PRENDRE (to take)	prends, prends, prend, pre*n*ons, pre*n*ez, pre*nn*ent	pris	prendrai
• DIRE (to say, tell)	dis, dis, dit, disons, *dites*, disent	dit	dirai
- LIRE (to read)	lis, lis, lit, lisons, lisez, lisent	*lu*	lirai
- ÉCRIRE (to write)	écris, écris, écrit, écrivons, écrivez, écrivent	écrit	écrirai
- RIRE (to laugh)	ris, ris, rit, *rions, riez*, rient	*ri*	rirai
◦ VENIR (to come)	*viens*, viens, vient, *venons*, venez, *viennent*	venu	*viendrai*
• VOIR (to see)	vois, vois, voit, voyons, voyez, voient	vu	*verrai*
• SAVOIR (to know)	sais, sais, sait, savons, savez, savent	su	*saurai*
• BOIRE (to drink)	bois, bois, boit, *buvons*, buvez, *boivent*	bu	boirai
• CROIRE (to believe)	crois, crois, croit, croyons, croyez, croient	cru	croirai

	Present Tense	**Past Part.**	**Future** (1st sing.)

- **SORTIR** (plus all *-ir* verbs with only one syllable in present sing.)[1]
  (to go out)

  sors, sors, sort, sorti sortirai
  sortons, sortez, sortent

- **OUVRIR** (plus all verbs ending in *-vrir* or *-frir*)[2]
  (to open)

  ouvre, ouvres, ouvre, *ouvert* ouvrirai
  ouvrons, ouvrez, ouvrent
  [present tense like *donner*]

- **CONDUIRE** (plus all verbs ending in *-uire*)[3]
  (to drive)

  conduis, conduis, conduit, conduit conduirai
  conduisons, conduisez,
  conduisent

- **RECEVOIR** (plus all verbs ending in *-cevoir*)[4]
  (to get)

  reçois, reçois, reçoit, *reçu* recevrai
  recevons, recevez, reçoivent

- **CRAINDRE** (plus all verbs ending in *-indre*, which replace the *-indre*
  (to fear)   with *-ins, -ins, -int, -ignons, -ignez, -ignent*)[5]

  crains, crains, craint, craint craindrai
  craignons, craignez, craignent

- **CONNAÎTRE** (plus all verbs ending in *-aître*)[6]
  (to know)

  connais, connais, connaît, connu connaîtrai
  connaissons, connaissez,
  connaissent

(1) including : dormir, s'endormir, mentir, partir, sentir, (se) servir.
(2) including : couvrir, découvrir, offrir, souffrir.
(3) including : construire, cuire, déduire, détruire, instruire, introduire,
     produire, réduire, séduire, traduire.
(4) including : apercevoir, concevoir, decevoir, percevoir.
(5) including : contraindre, éteindre, feindre, joindre, peindre, (se) plaindre, rejoindre, teindre.
(6) including : apparaître, disparaître, naître (except for p.p. *né*), paraître, reconnaître.

	Present Tense	**Past Part.**	**Future** (1st sing.)
• COURIR (to run)	*cours,* cours, *court,* courons, courez, courent	*couru*	*courrai*
• SUIVRE (to follow)	suis, suis, suit, suivons, suivez, suivent	*suivi*	suivrai
• VIVRE (to live)	vis, vis, vit, vivons, vivez, vivent	*vécu*	vivrai
• MOURIR (to die)	*meurs,* meurs, *meurt,* *mourons,* mourez, *meurent*	*mort*	*mourrai*
• ENVOYER (to send)	envoie, envoies, envoie, envoyons, envoyez, envoient	envoyé	*enverrai*
• VALOIR (to be worth)	vaux, vaux, vaut, valons, valez, valent	valu	vaudra

Two Impersonal verbs : Subject is always il (=it)

	Present	Imperfect	Passé Composé	Future
• FALLOIR (to be necessary)	il faut	il fallait	il a fallu	il faudra
• PLEUVOIR (to rain)	il pleut	il pleuvait	il a plu	il pleuvra

• S'ASSEOIR   **Past Participle** : *assis*
(to sit down)

		Present		Future
Either	je m'assieds	nous nous asseyons	je m'asseyerai
	tu t' assieds	vous vous asseyez	*or*
	il s' assied	ils s'asseyent	je m'assiérai
			or
or	je m'assois	nous nous assoyons	je m'assoirai
	tu t' assois	vous vous assoyez	
	il s' assoit	ils s'assoient	

	Present Tense	**Past Part.**	**Future** (1st sing.)
• BATTRE (to beat)	bats, bats, bat battons, battez, battent	battu	battrai
• FUIR (to flee)	fuis, fuis, fuit fuyons, fuyez, fuient	fui	fuirai
• HAÏR (to hate)	hais, hais, hait, haïssons, haïssez, haïssent	haï	haïrai
• PLAIRE (to please)	plais, plais, plaît, plaisons, plaisez, plaisent	*plu*	plairai
• ACQUÉRIR (to acquire)	*acquiers*, acquiers, *acquiert*, acquérons, acquérez, *acquièrent*	*acquis*	acquerrai
• CUEILLIR (to pick)	cueille, cueilles, cueille, cueillons, cueillez, cueillent [present tense like *donner*]	cueilli	cueill*e*rai
- ASSAILLIR (to attack)	assaille, assailles, assaille, assaillons, assaillez, assaillent [present tense like *donner*]	assailli	assaillirai
• RÉSOUDRE (to resolve)	résouds, résouds, résoud, résolvons, résolvez, résolvent	*résolu*	résoudrai
- COUDRE (to sew)	couds, couds, coud, cousons, cousez, cousent	*cousu*	coudrai
- MOUDRE (to grind)	mouds, mouds, moud, moulons, moulez, moulent	moulu	moudrai
• VAINCRE (to conquer)	vaincs, vaincs, vainc, vainquons, vainquez, vainquent	*vaincu*	vaincrai
• CONCLURE (to conclude)	conclus, conclus, conclut, concluons, concluez, concluent	conclu	conclurai
• MOUVOIR (to move)	meus, meus, meut, mouvons, mouvez, meuvent [similar to the pouvoir / vouloir / devoir group]	*mû*	mouvrai

- CROÎTRE   croîs, croîs, croît,   cr*û*   croîtrai
  (to increase)   croissons, croissez, croissent

- BOUILLIR   bous, bous, bout,   bouilli   bouillirai
  (to boil)   bouillons, bouillez, bouillent

- TRAIRE   trais, trais, trait,   trait   trairai
  (to milk)   trayons, trayez, traient

- VÊTIR   vêts, vêts, vêt,   *vêtu*   vêtirai
  (to clothe)   vêtons, vêtez, vêtent

- CLORE   clos, clos, clôt / clot,   clos   clorai
  (to close)   — , — , closent

INDEX OF IRREGULAR VERBS

A

abattre :   See *battre*, p.104
absoudre :   See *résoudre*, p.104
                 [except for p.p. - absous (m) absoute (f)]
abstenir :   See *venir*, p.101
abstraire :   See *traire*, p.105
accourir :   See *courir*, p.103
accroître :   See *croître*, p.105
accueillir :   See *cueillir*, p.104
acquérir :   p.104
adjoindre :   See *craindre*, p.102
admettre :   See *mettre*, p.101
aller :   p.100
apparaître :   See *connaître*, p.102
appartenir :   See *venir*, p.101
apercevoir :   See *recevoir*, p.102
apprendre :   See *prendre*, p.101
assaillir :   p.104
assentir :   See *sortir*, p.102
asservir :   Like *finir* (regular)
asseoir :   p.103
astreindre :   See *craindre*, p.102
atteindre :   See *craindre*, p.102
avoir :   p.100

B

battre :	p.104
boire :	p101
bouillir :	p.105
braire :	See *traire*, p.105

C

clore :	p.105
combattre :	See *battre*, p.104
commettre :	See *mettre*, p.101
complaire :	See *plaire*, p.104
comprendre :	See *prendre*, p.101
compromettre :	See *mettre*, p.101
concevoir :	See *recevoir*, p.102
conclure :	p.104
concourir :	See *courir*, p.103
conduire :	p.102
confire :	See *dire*, p.101
	[except for 2nd pl. of present - confisez]
connaître :	p.102
conquérir :	See *acquérir*, p.104
construire :	See *conduire*, p.102
contenir :	See *venir*, p.101
contraindre :	See *craindre*, p.102
contredire :	See *dire*, p.101
	[except for 2nd pl. of present - contredisez]
convaincre :	See *vaincre*, p.104
convenir :	See *venir*, p.101
corrompre :	Like *vendre* (regular)
	[except for 3rd sing. of present - corrompt]
coudre :	p.104
courir :	p.103
couvrir :	See *ouvrir*, p.102
craindre :	p.102
croire :	p.101
croître :	p.105
cueillir :	p.104
cuire :	See *conduire*, p.102

D

débattre :	See *battre*, p.104
decevoir :	See *recevoir*, p.102
découvrir :	See *ouvrir*, p.102
décrire :	See *écrire*, p.101
décroître :	See *croître*, p.105

dédire :	See *dire*, p.101
déduire :	See *conduire*, p.102
défaire :	See *faire*, p.101
déplaire :	See *plaire*, p.104
détruire :	See *conduire*, p.102
devenir :	See *venir*, p.101
devoir :	p.101
dire :	p.101
disparaître :	See *connaître*, p.102
dissoudre :	See *résoudre*, p.104
	[except for p.p. - dissous (m) dissoute (f)]
distraire :	See *traire*, p.105
dormir :	See *sortir*, p.102

E

écrire :	p.101
élire :	See *lire*, p.101
émettre :	See *mettre*, p.101
endormir :	See *sortir*, p.102
enfuir :	See *fuir*, p.104
enquérir :	See *acquérir*, p.104
entreprendre :	See *prendre*, p.101
entretenir :	See *venir*, p.101
entrevoir :	See *voir*, p.101
envoyer :	p.103
éprendre :	See *prendre*, p.101
équivaloir :	See *valoir*, p.103
éteindre :	See *craindre*, p.102
être :	p.100
exclure :	See *conclure*, p.104
extraire :	See *traire*, p.105

F

faillir :	See *assaillir*, p.104
faire :	p.101
falloir :	p.103
feindre :	See *craindre*, p.102
fuir :	p.104

H

haïr :	p.104

I

inclure :	See *conclure*, p.104
	[except for p.p. - inclus]

inscrire :	See *écrire*, p.101
instruire :	See *conduire*, p.102
interdire :	See *dire*, p.101
	[except for 2nd pl. of present - interdisez]
intervenir :	See *venir*, p.101
interrompre :	Like *vendre* (regular)
	[except for 3rd sing. of present - interrompt]
introduire :	See *conduire*, p.102

J
joindre :	See *craindre*, p.102

L
lire :	p.101
luire :	See *conduire*, p.102
	[except for p.p. - lui]

M
maintenir :	See *venir*, p.101
maudire :	Like *finir* (regular)
	[except for p.p. - maudit]
médire :	See *dire*, p.101
	[except for 2nd sing of present - médisez]
mentir :	See *sortir*, p.102
mettre :	p.101
moudre :	p.104
mourir :	p.103
mouvoir :	p.104

N
naître :	See *connaître*, p.102
	[except for p.p. - né]
nuire :	See *conduire*, p.102
	[except for p.p. - nui]

O
obtenir :	See *venir*, p.101
offrir :	See *ouvrir*, p.102
omettre :	See *mettre*, p.101
ouvrir :	p.102

P
paraître :	See *connaître*, p.102
parcourir :	See *courir*, p.103
parfaire :	See *faire*, p.101

partir :	See *sortir*, p.102
parvenir :	See *venir*, p.101
peindre :	See *craindre*, p.102
percevoir :	See *recevoir*, p.102
permettre :	See *mettre*, p.101
plaindre :	See *craindre*, p.102
plaire :	p.104
pleuvoir:	p.103
poursuivre :	See *suivre*, p.103
pourvoir :	See *voir*, p.101
	[except for future - pourvoirai, and past historic - pourvus]
pouvoir :	p.101
prédire :	See *dire*, p.101
	[except for 2nd pl. of present - prédisez]
prendre :	p.101
prévenir :	See *venir*, p.101
prévaloir :	See *valoir*, p.103
	[except subjunctive - prévale]
prévoir :	See *voir*, p.101
	[except future - prévoirai]
produire :	See *conduire*, p.102
promettre :	See *mettre*, p.101
promouvoir :	See *mouvoir*, p.104
	[except that p.p. has no accent]

R

rabattre :	See *battre*, p.104
recevoir :	p.102
reconnaître :	See *connaître*, p.102
recueillir :	See *cueillir*, p.104
réduire :	See *conduire*, p.102
rejoindre :	See *craindre*, p.102
relire :	See *lire*, p.101
reluire :	See *conduire*, p.102
	[except for p.p. - relui]
remettre :	See *mettre*, p.101
renaître :	See *connaître*, p.102
	[except that there is no p.p.]
renvoyer :	See *envoyer*, p.103
reproduire :	See *conduire*, p.102
requérir:	See *acquérir*, p.104
résoudre :	p.104
ressentir :	See *sortir*, p.102
retenir :	See *venir*, p.101

revenir :	See *venir*, p.101
revêtir :	See *vêtir*, p.105
rire :	p.101
rompre :	Like *vendre* (regular)
	[except for 3rd sing. of present - rompt]

S

satisfaire :	See *faire*, p.101
savoir :	p.101
secourir :	See *courir*, p.103
séduire :	See *conduire*, p.102
sentir :	See *sortir*, p.102
servir :	See *sortir*, p.102
sortir :	p.102
souffrir :	See *ouvrir*, p.102
soumettre :	See *mettre*, p.101
sourire :	See *rire*, p.101
souscrire :	See *écrire*, p.101
soutenir :	See *venir*, p.101
souvenir :	See *venir*, p.101
subvenir :	See *venir*, p.101
suffire :	See *dire*, p.101
	[except for 2nd pl. of present - suffisez, and p.p. - suffi]
suivre :	p.103
surprendre :	See *prendre*, p.101
survivre :	See *vivre*, p.103

T

taire :	See *plaire*, p.104
teindre :	See *craindre*, p.102
tenir :	See *venir*, p.101
traduire :	See *conduire*, p.102
traire :	p.105
transmettre :	See *mettre*, p.101
tressaillir :	See *assaillir*, p.104

V

vaincre :	p.104
valoir :	p.103
venir :	p.101
vêtir :	p.105
vivre :	p.103
voir :	p.101
vouloir :	p.101

APPENDIX B

VERBS EASILY CONFUSED

- *Écouter* – to listen   *Entendre* – to hear   *Attendre* – to wait

- *Raconter* – to tell, relate a story   *Rencontrer* – to meet   *Reconnaître* – to recognise

- *Pleuvoir* – to rain   *Pleurer* – to cry (weep)   *Crier* – to shout

- *Montrer* – to show   *Monter* – to get up on, climb

- *Regarder* – to look at, watch
  Voir – to see
  Avoir l'air – " to look" in the sense of "to seem",
    e.g. He looks sad. → Il a l'air triste.

- *Mourir* – to die   *Tuer* – to kill

- *Acheter* – to buy   *Vendre* – to sell

- *S'asseoir* – to sit down   → action : downward movement
  Être assis – to be sitting   → position : no movement

- To know : *Connaître* → knowing people or places
    Savoir → all other situations,
      e.g. to know something, to know how to do something

- To visit :   *Rendre visite à / Aller voir* → people
      Visiter → places

- To walk : *Marcher* → action of walking
    Se promener → to go for a walk
    Aller... à pied → to walk **to** some place

- To leave : *Quitter* (+ direct object) → to leave a place or person
    Partir → to leave i.e. to go away (without direct object)
    Laisser → to leave something behind

- Be careful with the spelling of regular *-er* verbs ending in *-ier*
  e.g. étudier, oublier, remercier, parier (to bet) etc.

  je remercie, tu remercies, il / elle remercie,
  nous remercions, vous remerciez, ils / elles remercient.

  The present tense singular of these verbs *sounds* like that of an *-ir* verb
  e.g. j'étudie le français.

APPENDIX C

-ER VERBS WITH VARIATIONS IN SPELLING

There are two groups of regular verbs with infinitives ending in *-er* that show slight changes in spelling in certain tenses. These changes are due to the two different ways of pronouncing both *c* and *g* in French, and to the system of stressing one particular syllable of a verb with a single consonant or *y* preceding the *-er* of the infinitive. The spelling variations are quite regular and logical, as the following pages seek to illustrate.

- (1) Regular verbs ending in *-ger* are spelt with an *-e-* after the *g*, whenever the verb ending begins with *a* or *o*.

    This happens in only three places : the 1st person plural of the present tense (**nous** part), all of the imperfect (except 1st and 2nd plural), all of the past historic (except 3rd plural).

    e.g. Manger :   (present)   nous mangeons
                    (imperfect) je mangeais, tu mangeais, il mangeait and ils mangeaient
                                  (**But** nous mangions, vous mangiez)

    Other *-ger* verbs include : arranger, bouger, changer, corriger, dégager, déranger, déménager, échanger, exiger, infliger, nager, neiger, obliger, partager, plonger, protéger, ranger, ronger, songer, soulager, voyager.

(2) Regular verbs ending in *-cer* have *ç* instead of *c* in those same three places.

    e.g. Commencer : (present)   nous commençons
                       (imperfect) je commençais, tu commençais, il commençait,
                                      ils commençaient.
                                      (**But** nous commencions, vous commenciez)

    Other *-cer* verbs include : annoncer, avancer, effacer, exercer, grincer, lancer, menacer, placer, remplacer, renoncer, sucer, tracer.

- Another spelling change affects regular verbs ending in e + consonant + er (e.g. acheter), é + consonant + er (e.g. espérer) or -yer (e.g. ennuyer). These verbs show a change of spelling whenever the ending has an unpronounced *e*. This occurs in four different parts of the verb :

    (i) all the singular and the 3rd plural of present tense indicative (i.e. je, tu, il, elle, ils, elles)
    (ii) all the singular and the 3rd plural of present subjunctive (same forms as present tense)
    (iii) all the future tense
    (iv) all the conditional.

The verbs fall into four different groups :

(1) *e* → *è,*   e.g. *Acheter*

Present :   j'achète, tu achètes, il / elle achète, ils / elles achètent
but no accent for 1st and 2nd persons plural
- nous achetons, vous achetez

Future :   j'achèterai, tu achèteras, etc.
Conditional :   j'achèterais, tu achèterais, etc.

No other parts of the verb show this spelling change,
e.g. j'ai acheté (passé composé), j'achetais (imperfect).

Other verbs showing the same spelling change as *acheter* include :
achever, chanceler, élever, enlever, geler, lever, mener, peler, peser, se promener, semer, soulever.

(2) *é* → *è,*   e.g. *Espérer*   (NB never any accent on the initial e)

Present :   j'espère, tu espères, il / elle espère, ils / elles espèrent
but no change for the 1st and 2nd persons plural
- nous espérons, vous espérez

Future :   j'espèrerai, tu espèreras, etc.
Conditional :   j'espèrerais, tu espèrerais, etc.

All other parts of the verb have the **é** of the infinitive,
e.g. j'ai espéré, (passé composé), j'espérais (imperfect).

Other verbs showing the same spelling change as *espérer* include :
céder, célébrer, considérer, exagérer, gérer, s'inquiéter, insérer, interpréter, lécher, libérer, posséder, préférer, protéger, référer, refléter, régler, répéter, révéler, suggérer.

(3) *Doubling of consonant*, e.g. *Appeler*

Present : j'appelle, tu appelles, il / elle appelle, ils / elles appellent
but no change (i.e. just one *l* as in infinitive)
– nous appelons, vous appelez

Future : j'appellerai, tu appelleras, etc.
Conditional : j'appellerais, tu appellerais, etc.

All other parts of the verb are like the infinitive,
e.g. j'ai appelé (passé composé), j'appelais (imperfect).

Other verbs which double either *l* or *t* include : étiqueter, jeter, se rappeler.

(4) *y → i*, e.g. *Ennuyer*

Present : j'ennuie, tu ennuies, il / elle ennuie, ils / elles ennuient
but the *y* is retained for the first and second persons plural
– nous ennuyons, vous ennuyez

Future : j'ennuierai, tu ennuieras, etc.
Conditional : j'ennuierais, tu ennuierais, etc.

All other parts of the verb retain the *y*,
e.g. j'ai ennuyé (passé composé), j'ennuyais (imperfect).

Other verbs which change *y* to *i* include :
aboyer, appuyer, balayer, effrayer, égayer, employer,
essayer, essuyer, nettoyer, noyer, payer.

(For verbs ending in *-ayer*, the change from *y* to *i* is optional.)

APPENDIX D

DEVOIR AND POUVOIR

These verbs present difficulties for two reasons :

(1) They are the French equivalent of a complicated range of auxiliary verbs in English (can, could, may, might, should, must, ought, etc.).

(2) Here in Ireland we do not use some of these words like *might* and *should* in the way an English person does, so that translating from standard English to French may require extra attention.

- **DEVOIR**   Basic meaning : *to have to*.

    I must   → present tense of devoir (je dois)
                             or future tense of devoir (je devrai)

    I must have   → passé composé of devoir (j'ai dû)

    I should
    I ought to   → conditional of devoir (je devrais)

    I should have
    I ought to have   → past conditional of devoir (j'aurais dû)

    I am to   → present tense of devoir (je dois)

    I was to   → imperfect tense of devoir (je devais)

- **POUVOIR**   Basic meaning : *to be able to*.

    I can
    I may   → present tense of pouvoir (je peux)

    I could   → conditional (je pourrais)   e.g. You could work harder.
                             or imperfect (je pouvais)   e.g. He admitted he couldn't open it.
                             or passé composé (j'ai pu)   e.g. When I tried, I could open it easily.

    I may have   → passé composé of pouvoir (j'ai pu)

    I might   → conditional of pouvoir (je pourrais)

    I could have
    I might have   → past conditional of pouvoir (j'aurais pu)

NB

(1) Devoir can often be replaced either by *être obligé de* (to have to) or by *falloir* (infinitive of *il faut*) with an indirect object pronoun.

    For example: il me faut = je dois
                     il nous fallait = nous devions
                     il lui faudra = il devra / elle devra

(2) Devoir can also mean "to owe" (i.e. to be in debt).

(3) Pouvoir is often not needed in French with verbs of seeing and hearing.

    For example: De ma chambre, on voit la flèche de l'église.
                     (From my room, you can see the church spire.)
                     Nous entendions le bruit de la circulation.
                     (We could hear the noise of the traffic.)

(4) *Savoir* and not pouvoir translates 'can' and 'could' when dealing with an acquired skill.

    For example: Il ne savait pas nager.
                     (He couldn't swim.)
                     Elle sait bien se défendre.
                     (She's quite able to look after herself.)

(5) *Savoir* is also found replacing pouvoir in careful literary French.

    For example: Je ne saurais [pas] répondre à votre question.
                     (I couldn't answer your question.)
                     Son explication a su nous rassurer.
                     (His explanation served to reassure us.)

APPENDIX E

EXPRESSIONS WITH AVOIR AND FAIRE

Avoir :
avoir chaud / froid	to be warm / cold
avoir faim / soif	to be hungry / thirsty
avoir raison / tort	to be right / wrong
avoir peur	to be afraid
avoir honte	to be ashamed
avoir sommeil	to be sleepy
avoir x ans	to be x years old
avoir de la chance	to be lucky
avoir besoin de	to need
avoir mal à —	to have a pain in —
avoir mal à faire	to have difficuluty doing
avoir envie de	to want to, to feel like
avoir beau [+ infinitive]	to do something in vain

Faire :
Weather Conditions :	Quel temps fait-il?
faire chaud / froid	to be warm / cold
faire beau	to be fine
faire mauvais	to be bad weather
faire du vent	to be windy
faire du soleil	to be sunny
faire du brouillard	to be foggy
faire de l'orage	to be stormy
faire jour	to be daylight
faire noir	to be dark
faire la vaisselle	to do the washing-up
faire la lessive	to do the washing / laundry
faire les devoirs	to do one's homework
faire le ménage	to do the housework
faire du bricolage	to do odd jobs
faire du repassage	to do the ironing
faire de la couture	to do sewing
faire de l'auto-stop	to hitch-hike
faire une promenade	to go for a walk
faire un pique-nique	to go for a picnic
faire un voyage	to go on a journey
faire semblant de	to pretend to

NB Il *a* chaud. → person
Il *fait* chaud → weather
Il *est* chaud → thing

Only with *être* does *chaud* agree as an adjective : l'eau est chaude.

APPENDIX F

NUMBERS

1 - 10 :   un, deux, trois, quatre, cinq, six, sept, huit, neuf, dix.

11 12 13 : onze douze treize
14 15 16 : quatorze quinze seize
17 18 19 : dix-sept dix-huit dix-neuf

20 30 40 50 60 : vingt trente quarante cinquante soixante

For *21, 31, etc., et* is used without a hyphen : 21 → vingt et un
                                                  51 → cinquante et un

All other numbers between *22* and *69* are hyphenated : *37* → trente-sept
                                                          45 → quarante-cinq

There is no single word in standard French for *70, 80* or *90*.

70 = 60 + 10 → soixante-dix.

80 = 4 x 20 → quatre-vingts (note the *-s*)

90 = 80 + 10 → quatre-vingt-dix

For *71 - 79* and *91 - 99* the words for *11 - 19* are used :

71 : soixante et onze   *91* : quatre-vingt-onze
72 : soixante-douze   *92* : quatre-vingt-douze
73 : soixante-treize   *93* : quatre-vingt-treize
74 : soixante-quatorze   *94* : quatre-vingt-quatorze
75 : soixante-quinze   *95* : quatre-vingt-quinze
76 : soixante-seize   *96* : quatre-vingt-seize
77 : soixante-dix-sept   *97* : quatre-vingt-dix-sept
78 : soixante-dix-huit   *98* : quatre-vingt-dix-huit
79 : soixante-dix-neuf   *99* : quatre-vingt-dix-neuf

81, 82 etc. are straightforward : quatre-vingt-un, quatre-vingt-deux, etc.

NB   - there is no *et* in *81* or *91*.
         - there is an *-s* in quatre-vingts (80) but not in *81 - 99*.

100 → cent   *107* → cent sept   *173* → cent soixante-treize

There is an *-s* on *cent* if the figure is a multiple of *100*, but not otherwise: *400* → quatre cents
415 → quatre cent quinze.

1,000 → mille (which never takes *-s*)   *3,000* → trois mille
Mil is used in dates only, e.g. *1993*: mil neuf cent quatre-vingt treize

APPENDIX G

EXPLETIVE NE WITH SUBJUNCTIVE

In a few of the subjunctive structures listed in Lessons 14 and 15, a *ne* is usually inserted before the verb in the subjunctive. This *ne*, which is a feature of correct formal French but not usually heard in the everyday spoken language, is found without *pas* and it has no negative value. It is called the *expletive ne*, where the word expletive means "redundant, fulfilling no purpose". It is found in the following cases :

(1) after verbs or conjunctions expressing fear :
   avoir peur que, craindre que (p.56)
   de peur que, de crainte que (p.58).
   e.g. Elle craint que tu *ne* sois mécontent.
   (She's afraid that you are dissatisfied.)

   Je vais rester à la maison de peur qu'il *ne* pleuve.
   (I'm going to stay at home for fear it will rain.)

(2) after *avant que* (before). See p.58.
   e.g. Tu devras les trouver avant qu'elle *ne* vienne.
   (You'll have to find them before she comes.)

(3) after *à moins que* (unless). See p.59.
   e.g. A moins que tout le monde *ne* rie, le clown n'est pas content.
   (Unless everybody laughs, the clown isn't happy.)

(4) after *éviter* (to avoid) when it is followed by *que* and a change of subject (following the same pattern as the verbs on pages 56 and 57).
   e.g. Il faut éviter qu'on *ne* vous voie.
   (You must avoid being seen by anybody.)

(5) after *sans que* (without) when the main verb of the sentence is negative. See p.59.
   e.g. On ne peut rien faire sans qu'elle *ne* s'en plaigne.
   (You can't do a thing without her complaining about it.)

APPENDIX H

USE OF REFLEXIVE VERBS TO TRANSLATE ENGLISH PASSIVE

This is quite a common construction in French and any examples you come across should be carefully noted.

For example: Cette erreur s'explique facilement.
(That mistake is easily explained.)

Cela ne se dit pas. (People don't say that.)

Il s'appelait Joseph. (He was called Joseph.)

Mes études se limitaient à ces trois romans.
(My study was limited to these three novels.)

Cela ne se fait plus en France.
(That is no longer done in France.)

Les pommes se vendent à deux francs la pièce.
(Apples are being sold at two francs each. / Apples cost two francs each.)

Le séminaire se tiendra les 2 et 3 juin.
(The seminar will be held on the second and third of June.)

Ils se sont vu interdire l'accès de la bibliothèque.
(They were refused admission to the library.)
i.e. *literally* "they saw themselves" being refused.

Le président s'est vu critiquer à cause de sa politique étrangère.
(The president was criticised for his foreign policy.)
i.e. *literally* "he saw himself" being criticised.

NB   **se faire** + infinitive and **se laisser** + infinitive

For example: Il s'est fait écraser. (He was run over. / He got run over.)
Elle s'est laissé tromper. (She was tricked. / She got tricked.)

These last structures imply that the subject was partly to blame for what happened.

APPENDIX I

ADDITIONAL EXAMPLES OF INVERSION

Lesson 10 shows how the order of subject before verb is reversed to denote a formal question. It also gives examples of inversion in the case of verbs of speech or thought which follow immediately after *direct speech*. Other examples of inversion include the following:

- Sentences beginning with certain adverbs or adverbial phrases such as: *peut-être* (perhaps), *à peine ... que ...* (scarcely), *sans doute* (probably), *aussi* (and so) require inversion.

    For example: Peut-être a-t-il oublié de venir.
    (Maybe he forgot to come.)

    A peine était-il rentré que le téléphone a sonné.
    (He had only just got back when the phone rang.)

    Nous avons manqué le train, aussi avons-nous pris un taxi.
    (We missed the train, and so we took a taxi.)

NB If *peut-être* follows the verb (normal position for an adverb) then there is no need for inversion. Sentences beginning with *peut-être* need not be inverted if **que** is inserted immediately after *peut-être*.

    For example: Il a peut-être oublié de venir.
    Peut-être qu'il a oublié de venir. (colloquial)

- Clauses beginning with the relative pronoun **que** may have inversion of subject and verb because the word order does not determine the meaning in French. (See Lesson 17 on the distinction between *qui* and *que*.)

    For example: Voilà le lion qu'a tué le chassseur.
    equivalent to Voilà le lion que le chasseur a tué.
    (That's the lion the hunter killed.)

    Il cherchait le portrait qu'avait peint son oncle.
    equivalent to Il cherchait le portrait que son oncle avait peint.
    (He was looking for the portrait his uncle had painted.)

APPENDIX J

ADDITIONAL TENSES

In total, there are **ten** tenses in the Indicative Mood in French : five **simple** tenses (where the verb consists of just one word) and five **compound** tenses (which are formed using an auxiliary verb).

Simple Tenses

Present :	je donne	(I give, I am giving, I do give)
Imperfect :	je donnais	(I was giving, I used to give)
Past Historic :	je donnai	(I gave)
Future :	je donnerai	(I shall give)
Conditional :	je donnerais	(I would give)

To form the following five compound tenses, the auxiliary verb is put in turn into each of the five simple tenses above.

Compound Tenses

Perfect (passé composé) :	j'ai donné	(I gave, I have given)
Pluperfect :	j'avais donné	(I had given)
Past Anterior :	j'eus donné	(I had given)
Future Perfect :	j'aurai donné	(I shall have given)
Past Conditional :	j'aurais donné	(I would have given)

Two of these tenses were not dealt with in the main part of this course :
the future perfect and the past anterior.

> The future perfect tense is a combination of the auxiliary verb in the future tense and the past participle. It translates "will have + past participle" or "shall have + past participle" in English, and is used to express the idea that an event will be completed at some point in the future.

For example: Il ira se promener quand *il aura nettoyé* la pièce.
(He will go for a walk when he has cleaned the room.)
[literally : when he will have cleaned]

Elle sera partie avant ton retour.
(She will have left before you get back.)

Quand tu viendras *ils se seront endormis*; j'en suis sûr.
(I'm sure they will have fallen asleep by the time you come.)

> The past anterior tense is a combination of the auxiliary verb in the past historic tense (see pp. 31 and 32) and the past participle. It has the same meaning as the pluperfect tense, i.e. "had + past participle" and is normally found in a sentence whose main verb is in the past historic tense.

It often follows conjunctions such as *après que* (after), *quand / lorsque* (when), *dès que / aussitôt que* (as soon as) and *à peine ... que* (scarcely ... than), indicating that one of the actions was fully completed before the other (expressed by the past historic) took place. Like the past historic, this tense is only found in formal narrative and never in informal or spoken French.

For example: Après qu'*il eut raconté* son histoire, *on l'enferma* dans la cellule.
                {past anterior}   {past historic}
        (After he had told his story, they locked him in the cell.)

        Nous quittâmes l'appartement dès qu'*Agnès se fut habillée*.
        {past historic}   {past anterior}
        (We left the flat as soon as Agnes had got dressed.)

        À peine *furent-ils sortis* qu'*il se mit* à pleuvoir.
             {past anterior}   {past historic}
        (Scarcely had they gone out than it started to rain.)

Note the inversion after *à peine* in the last example, as explained in Appendix I.

There are **four** tenses in the Subjunctive Mood in French, of which the two that are used in everyday spoken French, namely the present subjunctive and the perfect subjunctive, are explained in Lesson 14. The remaining two are only found in formal, literary French and nowadays the 3rd person singular is the only part likely to be used.

> The imperfect subjunctive is formed by removing the final **letter** of the past historic 1st person singular and adding the endings : -sse, -sses, -^t, -ssions, -ssiez, -ssent.

For example: Bien qu'*il vînt* souvent les voir, il avait toujours peur d'eux.
        (Although he often came to see them, he was afraid of them the whole time.)

        Avant qu'*il ne fît* la connaissance de Sophie, sa femme l'avait déjà rencontrée deux fois.
        (Before he met Sophie, his wife had already met her twice.)

> The pluperfect subjunctive is a combination of the imperfect subjunctive of the auxiliary verb and the past participle.

For example: Bien qu'*il fût arrivé* à l'heure, le professeur le gronda.
        (Although he had come on time, the teacher scolded him.)

APPENDIX K

DEMONSTRATIVE PRONOUNS AND POSSESSIVE PRONOUNS

There are several other types of pronoun in French apart from those mentioned in Lessons 16, 17 and 18. Two of them are used in situations where the word *one* is used in English, e.g. the *one* with the red cover, this *one*, my *one*, their *one*.

DEMONSTRATIVE PRONOUNS

	Masculine	Feminine
Singular	*Celui*	*Celle*
Plural	*Ceux*	*Celles*

These pronouns are normally used in one of three ways :

- celui *de*

    For example: Ce livre est difficile mais celui de Marie ne l'est pas.
                 (This book is difficult but Mary's one isn't.)

                Mes enfants ne ressemblent pas à ceux de mon frère.
                (My children don't look like my brother's.)

- celui + *qui / que / dont*

    For example: J'aime mieux ce prof que celle qui enseigne les maths.
                 (I prefer this teacher to the one who teaches Maths.)

                Prends cette montre; celle que tu as choisie avance.
                (Take this watch; the one you picked is fast.)

- celui-*ci*, celui-*là*

    For example: Elle vient d'acheter deux robes; celle-ci est jolie mais celle-là ne me plaît pas.
                 (She's just bought two dresses; this one is pretty but I don't like that one.)

                Ces fleurs-ci sont assez rares, tandis qu'on voit celles-là dans tous les jardins.
                (These flowers are quite rare, but those ones can be seen in every garden.)

POSSESSIVE PRONOUNS

	Singular		Plural	
	(masc.)	(fem.)	(masc.)	(fem.)
mine, my one(s) yours, your one(s)	le *mien* le *tien*	la *mienne* la *tienne*	les *miens* les *tiens*	les *miennes* les *tiennes*
{ his, his one(s) } { hers, her one(s) }	le *sien*	la *sienne*	les *siens*	les *siennes*
ours, our one(s) yours, your one(s) theirs, their one(s)	le *nôtre* le *vôtre* le *leur*	la *nôtre* la *vôtre* la *leur*	les *nôtres* les *vôtres* les *leurs*	

For example: Notre voiture est blanche alors que *la leur* est noire.
(Our car is white but theirs is black.)

Les parents de Philippe habitent à Paris et *les miens* en Angleterre.
Les tiens, où habitent-ils ?
(Philip's parents live in Paris and mine in England. Where do yours live ?)

Véronique et moi, nous sommes cousins; mon père et *le sien* sont frères.
(Veronica and I are cousins; my father and hers are brothers.)

NB (i) The circonflex accent in *nôtre(s)* and *vôtre(s)* distinguishes these pronouns from notre and votre (possessive adjectives : p.79)

(ii) *Leur* (indirect object pronoun = to them : p.63) never takes -s.
Leur (possessive adjective = their : p.79) takes -s if it precedes a plural noun.
le *leur*, la *leur*, les *leurs* (possessive pronoun = theirs : above).

INDEX

à
- + definite article 86
- + object 72, 73, 95
- following certain verbs 95
- following some adjectives 96

About 93

Active Voice
- meaning in English 11

Adjective 76-80
- defined 7
- agreement : regular 76
- agreement : irregular 76-78
- position 78
- position changes meaning 79
- possessive adjective 79-80
- used as adverb 89

Adverb
- defined 7-8
- formation 88
- irregular adverbs 88

Afin de / que 58

After 52 - 53, 58

Agreement
- of adjectives 76 - 79
- of past participle 18, 81-83
- of p.p. in passive voice 49
- of present participle 51

Aller + Infinitive 35

Although 59

Après 58
- + perfect infinitive 52-53

Après que 53, 58

Article 85 - 87
- defined 8
- definite article 8, 85 - 86
- indefinite article 8, 85
- partitive article 8, 86-87

Aucun 25-26

Auquel / À laquelle 67

Auxiliary verb 14 -16, 122

Avant de 58

Avant que 58

Avoir
- forming passé composé 15-16
- expressions with avoir 117

Bien que 59

Ce / Cette 77
Ce qui / Ce que 69
Celui / Celle 124
Chez 71
Combien de
- direct object preceding 82
Commands
  See "Imperative" or
    "Verbs of command"
Comparative
- of adjective 89-90
- of adverb 90
Complex Inversion 42-43
Composite Subjects
- use of stressed pronoun 71
Compound Tense 14, 122
Compound Verb 100
Concessive Clauses
  See "Although"
Conditional Perfect
  See "Past Conditional"
Conditional Tense
- meaning in English 11
- formation 36
- some uses 36
- with si 38-39
Conjugations of Verbs 14
Conjunction
- defined 8
- followed by subjunctive 58-59
- of time 58
- of purpose 58
Continuous Present 15
De
- + definite article 86
- + object 72, 73, 96
- following certain verbs 95-96
- following some adjectives 96-97
De façon que 58-59
De sorte que 58-59
Definite Article 8, 85-86
Depuis 45-47
- with continuing event 45
- with completed event 46
- with negative 46
- alternatives 45-46

- depuis que 47
Devoir 101, 115-116
Direct Object 61-62, 64-65
- agreement with direct object preceding verb 81- 83
Direct Speech
- inversion following 43
Disjunctive Pronoun
  See "Stressed Pronoun"
Dont 68
Duquel 67
En
- as object pronoun 72-73
- + present participle 51-52
- + countries 92
Est-ce que 40, 42-43
Être
- forming passé composé 18
Être sur le point de 35
Expletive ne
- with subjunctive 119
Expressions of quantity 87
Faire
- expressions with faire 117
Falloir 56-57, 103
For
- pour / pendant 93
- depuis 45-47
From 92, 98
Future Perfect Tense 122
Future Tense
- meaning in English 11
- formation / endings 34
- some uses 34-35
- with si 38-39

Gerund 51
Il faut 56-57
Immediate Future 35
Imperative 27
- of reflexive verbs 27
- irregular imperatives 27
- negative 27
- with object pronouns 74-75
Imperfect Tense
- meaning in English 11

- formation / endings 22
- when to use 22-24
Impersonal Verbs
- + subjunctive 56
In 92
Indefinite Article 8, 85
Indicative Mood
(in contrast to Subjunctive) 54, 122
Indirect Object 61, 63-64, 72-73
- problems with passive 50
Infinitive 14
- verbs followed by inf. 98
- following prepositions 52, 94-96
- other uses (note) 52, 57
- to make negative 25
Interrogative Forms
See "Questions"
Intransitive Verbs 18
Inversion
- for questions 40-43
- after direct speech 43
- other uses 121
Inverted Questions 40-43
Irregular Verbs
- which parts to learn 14, 100
- irregular verb lists 100-110
- irregular imperatives 27
- irregular subjunctives 54-55
Jusqu'à ce que 58
Leave (verb) 111
Lequel / Laquelle 67
Meilleur 90
- meilleur or mieux ? 90
Mieux 90
Ne
- with que 25-26
- with subjunctive 119
Negative 25-26
- negative questions 40-42
Noun
- defined 7
Numbers 118
Object 61
- direct 61-62, 64-65
- indirect 63-65, 72-73
- following à 72-73

- following de 72-73
- position 74-75
On (French) 49-50
On (English) 93
Order of Object Pronouns 74-75
Où
- as relative pronoun 68
Participles
- past 15-16
- present 51-52
Partitive Article 86-87
Parts of Speech 7 - 9
Passé Composé 15
- verbs with avoir 15-16
- verbs with être 18-20
- reflexive verbs 20
- when to use 22-24
- to make negative 25, 26
- question form 41-42
Passé Simple
See "Past Historic Tense"
Passive Voice 48-50
- meaning in English 11-12
Past Anterior Tense 122
Past Conditional Tense
- meaning in English 11
- formation 38
Past Historic Tense
- formation / endings 31-32
- when to use 31
Past Infinitive
See "Perfect Infinitive"
Past Participle 16
- agreement 18, 81-83
Past Subjunctive
See "Subjunctive Mood - perfect"
Past Tenses
- meanings in English 11-12
- deciding which to use 22-24
Pendant 93
Pendant que 51
Perfect Infinitive 52-53
Perfect Tense
- meaning in English 11
See "Passé Composé"
Peut-être 121

Pluperfect Tense
- meaning in English 11
- formation 29
- some uses 29-30
Position of Object Pronouns 74-75
Possessive Adjective 79-80
Pour
- + infinitive 99, 58
- + time 93
Pour que 58
Pouvoir 101, 115-116
Preposition 92-99
- defined 8
- after verb of motion 94
- + relative pronoun 67
- + stressed pronoun 71
- repetition of 97
Present Participle 51-52
Present Tense
- meaning in English 11
- formation / endings 14-15
Pronoun
- defined 8
- demonstrative pronoun 124
- personal pronoun 8
- possessive pronoun 125
- relative pronoun 8, 66-69
- object pronoun 61-65, 72-75
- stressed pronoun 71

Que (relative pronoun) 66-67
Quel / Quelle
- direct object preceding 82
Quelque chose + à / de 97
Questions 40-43
Qui 66-67
Quoique 59
Reflexive Verbs
- present tense 19
- passé composé 20
- imperative 27
- question form 41-42
- to translate passive 120
Relative Pronoun 8, 66-69
- summary of forms 70
- following preposition 67
- followed by subjunctive 59

Rien
- + à / de 97
Sans 59
Sans que 59
Si
- tense combinations 38-39
- si meaning "whether" 39
Since 45-47
Stressed Pronoun 71
Subject 61
Subjunctive Mood 54-60
- summary of uses 60
- present subjunctive :
  formation / endings 54
- imperfect subjunctive 122
- irregular subjunctives 54-55
- perfect subjunctive 55
- pluperfect subjunctive 122
- standing alone 55
- following verbs 56-57
- following conjunctions 58-59
- following relative pronoun 59-60

Superlative
- of adjective 89-90
- followed by subjunctive 59
- of adverb 90
Tenses
- meanings in English 11-12
- deciding which past tense
  to use 22-24
This / That / These / Those 77
To
- + town / country 92
- + definite article 86
Tout
- agreement
  (as adjective) 78
- + relative pronoun 69
Transitive Verbs
 (mentioned) 19
Until 58
Venir de 30-31
Verb
- defined 7
- tenses 11-12

Verbs conjugated with être 18
Verbs easily confused 111
Verbs of command
- + subjunctive 56
Verbs of emotion
- + subjunctive 56
Verbs expressing lack of
            knowledge
- + subjunctive 56
Verbs of motion with prep. 94
Verbs of seeing and hearing 52
Verbs : spelling variations 112-114
Visit (verb) 111
Walk (verb) 111
Whether 39
With 93
Without 59
Y 72, 73